MW00626082

Baptists in Transition:
Individualism and Christian Responsibility

Winthrop S. Hudson

Baptists in Transition:
Individualism and Christian Responsibility

Foreword by Robert T. Handy

Judson Press ® Valley Forge

BAPTISTS IN TRANSITION
Copyright © 1979
Judson Press, Valley Forge, PA 19481

All rights reserved. No part of this publication may be reproduced, stored in a retrieval system, or transmitted in any form or by any means, electronic, mechanical, photocopying, recording, or otherwise, without the prior permission of the copyright owner, except for brief quotations included in a review of the book.

Permission is gratefully acknowledged for use of the following articles from *Foundations:*
"Prolegomena to a Theology of Church Order," vol. 8 (April, 1965), pp. 101-116.
"The Associational Principle Among Baptists," vol. 1 (January, 1958), pp. 10-23.
"The Pastoral Ministry: Call and Ordination," vol. 5 (July, 1962), pp. 238-249.
"Stumbling into Disorder," vol. 1 (April, 1958), pp. 45-71.
"The Divergent Careers of Southern and Northern Baptists: A Study in Growth," vol. 16 (April–June, 1973), pp. 171-183.
Permission is also acknowledged from Judson Press for use of the following selections:
"Baptists, the Pilgrim Fathers, and the American Revolution," from *Baptists and the American Experience,* edited by James E. Wood, Jr., Copyright 1976, pp. 25-38.
"Shifting Patterns of Church Order in the Twentieth Century," from *Baptist Concepts of the Church,* edited by Winthrop S. Hudson, Copyright 1959, pp. 196-218.

Library of Congress Cataloging in Publication Data
Hudson, Winthrop Still, 1911-
    Baptists in transition.
    Includes bibliographical references and index.
    1. Baptists—Doctrinal and controversial works—
Baptist authors—Collected works.   2. Baptists—United
States—History—Collected works.   I. Title
BX6331.2.H76   262'.06   79-18515
ISBN 0-8170-0852-7

The name JUDSON PRESS is registered as a trademark in the U.S. Patent Office. Printed in the U.S.A. ✆

Contents

Foreword

by Robert T. Handy

For American Baptists, Winthrop S. Hudson has long played a distinguished role as a critical historical interpreter, probing boldly into the Baptist past in order to identify the various strands in our history that have come into collision. His ability to discern with penetrating clarity the complex history of a people devoted to freedom and to congregational polity stems in part from his broad understanding of the whole sweep of church history, especially in England and America, as is evidenced in such of his books as *The Great Tradition of the American Churches* (1953, 1970) and the two editions of *Religion in America* (1965, 1973). For the task of defining the tensions in thought and practice that have long plagued Baptists in the United States, however, Hudson chose the historical essay as the instrument best suited. The seven essays that follow were written over a period of years. Five of them appeared in *Foundations: A Baptist Journal of History and Theology;* one in a book he also edited, *Baptist Concepts of the Church,* and another in the Bicentennial book, *Baptists and the American Experience,* edited by James E. Wood, Jr. These writings by Hudson have become major contributions of the study of the Baptist past and present, are cited often in articles and books, and have played a role in the reorganization of American Baptist Churches in the 1970s.

The first three of the essays as they appear in this volume are primarily analytical, probing the deep tensions in Baptist life between a churchly understanding of Christian faith and a highly individualistic one. His exposition of the historical development of the associational principle has made an indelible impression on historians and ecclesiologists, and the student of Baptist life who does not take it into account is simply out of date. But these analytical articles also contain not a little narrative, for Hudson's work is grounded in a broad understanding of Baptist origins and development. Before any of these writings appeared, there were two articles in *The Chronicle,* the historical quarterly that preceded *Foundations,* that show some of the groundwork on which his later contributions were based. "Baptists Were Not Anabaptists" showed definitively that the Baptists arose historically out of English Puritanism in the early seventeenth century and not out of continental Anabaptism.[1] "Themes for Research in Baptist History" displayed vast bibliographical knowledge and opened up avenues of research and study that have since been fruitfully followed by Hudson and many others.[2] Such foundational articles show an appreciation of the importance of narrative historical interpretation; the bold analytical approach of the first part of this book arises out of a firm grasp of the overall story and brings it into sharper focus by its deliberate selection of critical junctures. The analyst is also narrator.

The second part of the book continues the critical probing but with greater narrative intent and content; major chapters in the Baptist story that Hudson's work so richly illuminates are told in a carefully documented way. Though each essay focuses on a particular theme and period, together they provide the reader with significant interpretations of crucial developments in Baptist history over a span of two centuries.

In the chapters that follow, and also in his introduction to *Baptist Concepts of the Church,* Hudson has highlighted the original churchly pattern of Baptist faith and ecclesiology as developed especially by the English Particular Baptists and adopted by the Philadelphia Baptist Association, a pattern which "did determine the basic initial orientation of the denomination both in doctrine and in polity."[3] The position, based on an exegesis of relevant biblical passages and buttressed by theological reflection, was one which held in dynamic tension congregational polity and the associational principle, and which worked out a responsible "middle way" between congregational autonomy and centralized church authority at the level of the association (or a convention as an "association of associations"). Hudson explains how three developments affected this pattern: the emergence of an evangelical interpretation of Baptist faith and life during the Great Awakening, the impact of the pronounced individualism of the Baptist Separates (especially Isaac Backus) of New England, and the stance of the "Jeffersonian Baptists" (especially John Leland) who were deeply informed by currents of Enlightenment thought.

These developments prepared the way for the acceptance of radically individualistic interpretations of Baptist principles in the nineteenth century. Thus many were led to neglect or forget the earlier principles of responsible associationalism. While the consequences of this shift among Baptists are carefully probed in these writings, especially in the famous essay on "Stumbling into Disorder," not a great deal is said about the combination of intellectual and environmental forces that led to the uncritical adoption of radical individualism by so many Baptists in the early nineteenth century. It has been characteristic of Winthrop Hudson to encourage students and colleagues to pursue avenues of investigation and interpretation to which he has pointed; he helped to encourage me to probe into the reasons why many American Christians, Baptists among them, were drawn into the patterns of individualism that so dominated American life in the nineteenth century. A summary of these reasons may help us to see why so many Baptists were pulled away from their original orientations and were drawn as by a powerful magnet to the highly individualistic and localistic positions which have caused serious difficulties in dealing relevantly with the realities of twentieth-century ecumenical and cultural developments.

I

A number of disparate forces worked together in the late eighteenth and early nineteenth centuries to thrust what Alfred North White-head called a "gospel of individualism" into the mainstream of American thought and life. While this whole story could fill several volumes, attention to five of these forces provides it major outlines.

1. The emphasis within Puritanism on the necessity of an intense religious experience focused attention on the individual and stirred vigorous debates on the role of "preparation" for salvation. In early Puritan Calvinism the objective and subjective aspects of faith were held in creative balance by the movement's heavy stress on divine sovereignty and its high doctrine of the church; with the passage of time these emphases faded somewhat, and the individual received greater attention in theological thought. In a provocative article, Ellwood Johnson has suggested that an important root of individualism (a word apparently coined by De Tocqueville in the nineteenth century) lies in Calvinist preparationist thought and in the evangelical Calvinism stimulated by the Great Awakening.[4] With their own rootage in Puritanism

and in evangelical Calvinism, Baptists were deeply involved in these trends, and many were thus theologically prepared to look congenially on the philosophy of individualism as it emerged in the late eighteenth and early nineteenth centuries.

2. A second factor leading to the triumph of individualism was the Enlightenment. The revolutions in thought and government which were in large part inspired by the currents we label "Enlightenment" sought to free individuals from the shackles of despotism, inequality, ignorance, and superstition. The Enlightenment philosophy, enshrined to a considerable extent in the basic documents of the new American republic, declared that freed natural reason probing the record of past human experience would find the solution to the major problems of history. If only the individual were freed, it was insisted, the evils of the past would melt away. Looking back, we see with sorrow how selective was the range of individuals who were to be freed, but the ideal of the free individual was nonetheless exalted.

Certain of the key themes of Enlightenment thought also made considerable impression on Christian thought and life, in some quarters more than others. Some of the emphases of the Age of Reason were secularized forms of Christian doctrines, and so church leaders could often agree with them, as far as they went. A good deal of secularized Calvinism seeped into American Enlightenment thought through such channels as the works of John Locke and the Scottish commonsense philosophers. John Witherspoon, for example, the conspicuous president of the College of New Jersey at Princeton, a Scotsman who was one of the country's leading teachers of moral philosophy, could promptly sign the Declaration as one of his first acts on joining Continental Congress. Certainly as a Presbyterian minister and theologian he could say much more about God than the brief references to "nature's God" that Jefferson wrote into that Enlightenment document; but insofar as it went, Jefferson's statement was not inconsistent with his theology. More importantly, Witherspoon, like many other Christians, had tired of alignments of churches with oppressive political and economic systems and welcomed the concern of the Enlightenment for freedom. One of the most conspicuous figures to bring together a fiery pietism with a rationalist spirit was a Baptist, John Leland, an ardent supporter of Jefferson and an indefatigable advocate of religious and civil freedom for individuals. While few Baptists were as committed to what one contemporary called Leland's "almost mad devotion to politics," many were as emphatic as he was about the importance of the freedom of the individual.[5]

3. A third force which was instrumental in the triumph of individualism in the United States was quite different, for what we call Romanticism was in part a reaction against the Enlightenment. In fact, there were a number of movements of the late eighteenth and early nineteenth centuries which we often lump under the term "Romanticism," movements which were protesting against Enlightenment emphases on reason and order. Romanticists of various types objected to the way the Age of Reason had interpreted human experience; they found it too narrow, rational, and cold—not sufficiently fused with human feeling and warmth. Paul Tillich often pointed out that the theological root principle of Romantic movements was the awareness of the presence of the infinite in everything finite.[6] It was this principle that undergirded the protest against the rationalistic and mechanistic world views that characterized so much Enlightenment thought, and that led Romantics to magnify the individual as embodying something unique and divine. Thus Romanticism, though in many ways a reaction against the Enlightenment, in its own way also called for the freedom of the individual. At this important point the two movements, so different from one another, reinforced each other and played important roles in the rise of individualism.

When Romanticism is mentioned, we often think first of Europe and the English poets, but long ago Ralph H. Gabriel explained that a "popular Romanticism" became a powerful force in the thought and feeling of Americans in the first half of the nineteenth century, giving to that period much of its character. Observing that "there is an alchemy at work in every climate of opinion that tends to dissolve inconsistencies and to establish fundamental agreements," he explained that for that period

> romanticism provided the solvent. It permeated the arts and literature. It expressed itself in the South in the cult of chivalry and in the romantic nationalism of the dream of the confederate States of America. It created the fundamental similarities between religious and secular thinking.[7]

One of the most important channels for popular Romanticism was evangelical religion, especially in the revivals and camp meetings of the Second Great Awakening, in which Baptists played conspicuous roles and through which their devotion to individualism was further intensified.

4. A fourth factor in the spread of the gospel of individualism was environmental rather than ideological: the fact of the frontier. After long discussion, so-called "frontier theses" which sought to *explain* American development in terms of the frontier have long since been rejected, but there is no reason to go to the other extreme and fail to give the frontier its proper place—especially in the history of individualism. In the great westward movements of the nineteenth century, individuals were indeed often dependent on their own resources for sheer survival and frequently became fiercely proud of their independence. The sense of individual competency, self-sufficiency, and freedom was in general much strengthened by frontier experiences. The myths about the nature and opportunities of the frontier often outran the realities, but both as fact and myth the frontier contributed much to the developing philosophy of individualism. To be sure, frontier settlements and villages also impressed certain attitudes of conformity on people, as T. Scott Miyakawa has demonstrated in his thoughtful book, *Protestants and Pioneers: Individualism and Conformity on the American Frontier.* He showed how some of the social pressures of frontier society served, quite paradoxically, to insure that individuals held the right beliefs respecting individualism![8] But there is ample documentation in his and other works of the strongly individualistic qualities of frontier life in both belief and reality. The importance of their frontier experiences for Baptists has been suggested by many historians; the denomination's commitment to individualism was strengthened by such experiences.[9]

5. The fifth source of the popular philosophy of individualism to be mentioned in this hasty summary was the widespread acceptance in American life of classical liberal political economy, with its heavy insistence of the freedom of the individual economic person, the rights of private property, and the freedom of the marketplace from political control. Words can change meaning over time: in the early nineteenth century, against the background of mercantilism, this was indeed *liberal* economic teaching; the dynamics of history have turned what was once liberal teaching into conservative economic doctrine. The "classical liberal" economic position became standard doctrine in American church and academic life. The views were given a pietistic adaptation, largely by the Scottish commonsense philosophers. Henry F. May has declared that "American scholars worked out a school of political economy which might well be labeled clerical laissez

faire. For at least a generation and in many institutions far longer, this body of doctrine dominated American economic teaching."[10] On the political side, such individualistic attitudes reinforced concepts of minimal government, as in Jefferson's phrase, "he governs best who governs least," and in Emerson's "the less government we have the better." The sense of corporate responsibility for human welfare was thus largely dissolved, and major currents in economic, political, and social thought supported the trend toward individualism. Some prominent Baptists played influential roles in the triumph of "clerical laissez faire," notably Francis Wayland, a leading moral philosopher and college president, whose powerful influence in the history of Baptists in America is traced in one of the essays that follow.

II

This listing of five forces of varying kinds that converged to emphasize individual freedom in the early nineteenth century is intended to be suggestive and not exhaustive, but it may help us to understand why the philosophy of individualism cut so deeply into American culture and institutional life. Many writers, Hudson conspicuous among them, have explained how the gospel of individualism penetrated American church life, especially of the evangelical churches, eroding earlier corporate Christian concerns for the larger structures of the church and of national life. For many, the gospel of Christ and the gospel of individualism seemed virtually to coincide.

One of the most unambiguous and widely influential statements of the philosophy of individualism was by that prominent Baptist minister and educator already cited, Francis Wayland. In an oft-reprinted and much studied work, Wayland said:

> Every human being is, by his constitution, a separate, and distinct, and complete system, adapted to all the purposes of self-government, and responsible, separately, to God, for the manner in which his powers are employed. . . . He need assign no other reason for his conduct, than his own free choice. Within this limit, he is still responsible to God; but . . . he is not responsible *to man*, nor *is man responsible for him*.[11]

It was Wayland who pressed a corollary of this doctrine of radical individualism: localism. He distrusted forms of church organization beyond the local scene, for the individual might be committed to a position to which one had not consented. He believed that "each christian church, as such, is incapable of representation," and that "each church is therefore as essentially independent of every other, as though each one were the only church in christendom."[12] Many others went along with such teaching; those under the spell of individualism and its corollary, localism, saw the church essentially as a local voluntary society of Christians who could not make laws for each other nor impinge on one another's freedom in any way.

The deep penetration of individualism and localism in Baptist life and thought has meant that variant interpretations of the denomination, arising out of different periods, have been in conflict. The work of Hudson and others has illuminated the tensions of our history, allowing us to have a fuller understanding of our past—and hence of our present as we move toward the future. Of course, the experience of the nineteenth century is not to be rejected; it is to be understood for insights that can be reinterpreted and appropriated for today's—and tomorrow's—realities. George Hendry once paid tribute to what some nineteenth-century persons saw clearly when he asserted that "the communion of saints is not safe without an element of recalcitrant, rebellious, and intractable individualism."[13] Perhaps now we are prepared to hear what Orestes A. Brownson called attention to as early as 1842 in noting the difference between individual*ism* and individual*ity:* "Community without individuality is *tyranny*, the fruits of which are oppression, degradation and immobility, the synonym of death. Individuality without community is *individualism*, the fruits of which are dissolution, isolation, selfishness, disorder, anarchy, confusion, war."[14] Individuality is quite different from individualism, for it is nourished in community, draws strength from community, and contributes to its ongoing life.

Among Baptist voices recalling the tradition back from excessive individualism to Christian responsibility, Hudson's has been especially notable. These essays have had a significant influence in the reorganization of the American Baptist Convention into the American Baptist Churches in the 1970s. The final report of the Study Commission on Denominational Structure (SCODS) explained its task as follows:

> One of the principal mandates to the Commission was to develop a more representative structure at the national level with clear lines of accountability. This mandate came through loud and clear at the 1968 Boston Convention which created SCODS, and it was repeatedly

affirmed at the listening conferences held around the country in the months that followed. The mandate reflected more than a decade of writings by numerous scholars concerning the structure and polity of the A.B.C.[15]

Highly prominent among the "numerous scholars" and a leader in encouraging others in the work of reinterpretation was Winthrop Hudson. In "A Preamble to a Proposal for Restructure of the American Baptist Convention," another distinguished Baptist historian, Robert G. Torbet, author of the standard overall work, *A History of the Baptists,* after referring to a book which Hudson coauthored, summarized a major trend in ecclesiological thought among American Baptists:

> Accordingly, we have come to see the need for a delegated body to increase the ability of elected representatives of the congregations to hear and to understand each other and so be able to act responsibly under the guidance of the Holy Spirit. Such a shift in polity is from the society concept to the churchly concept. Behind the churchly concept is the assumption that there are times when quite properly the congregations need to speak together as a denomination on theological and doctrinal issues as well as to engage in joint action in mission. We need, therefore, to recognize that we, as a denomination, are as truly a church within the Body of Christ as any one of the congregations in which we hold our membership.[16]

Hudson has been a primary leader of thought behind this shift from society to churchly concept. Not only in the essays that appear here, but also in his work with students and colleagues, as former president of the American Baptist Historical Society and an editor of *Foundations,* and as contributor to many conferences and gatherings, Hudson has been a major force behind the reshaping of a denomination. He has not been directly involved in the details of reorganization, and one suspects he would not approve all that has happened. His has been a foundational role of contributing significantly to a shift in the climate of opinion that has made change possible.

One of the following essays, "The Associational Principle Among Baptists," appeared in the very first issue of *Foundations.* In that same historic number was an article by the late Daniel Day Williams, "The Mystery of the Baptists." A member of the United Church of Christ, Williams was associated with H. Richard Niebuhr and James M. Gustafson in a study of theological education. During a year of extensive research, Williams focused some of his scholarly attention on the Baptists. In summarizing his findings, he reported:

But I came to believe during this year of reflection on our church life that the probing of the mystery of the Baptists will have to go deeper than the tracing of such cultural and political elements. Here is a form of the Christian community which rests upon an experience of the Gospel which is personal, rather easily intelligible, vividly symbolized, calling for personal dedication, and open to the promptings of the Spirit. The Baptists seem to prove that the Christian church can live and grow as a personal fellowship based on a directly shared experience, provided it is interpreted through a commonly accepted language of Scriptural symbols. Other forms of the Christian church which depend more upon creed, liturgy or a highly articulated ecclesiastical organization are not the only sources of the unity of Christian groups. The power of the Spirit can produce the fellowship.[17]

Winthrop Hudson has trusted in that power as he carries on his work as minister, historian, teacher, thinker, and author.

NOTES

[1] *The Chronicle,* vol. 16, no. 4 (1953), pp. 171-179.

[2] *Ibid.,* vol. 17, no. 1 (1954), pp. 3-23.

[3] Winthrop S. Hudson, ed., *Baptist Concepts of the Church* (Valley Forge: Judson Press, 1959), p. 21.

[4] Ellwood Johnson, "Individualism and the Puritan Imagination," *American Quarterly,* vol. 22 (Summer, 1970), pp. 231-234.

[5] On Leland, see Edwin S. Gaustad, "The Backus–Leland Tradition," in Hudson, ed., *Baptist Concepts of the Church,* pp. 106-134; see especially p. 133.

[6] Paul Tillich, *Perspectives on 19th and 20th Century Protestant Theology,* ed. Carl E. Braaten (New York: Harper & Row, Publishers, 1967), chap. 3.

[7] Ralph H. Gabriel, "Evangelical Religion and Popular Romanticism in Early Ninteenth-Century America," *Church History,* vol. 19 (1950), p. 45.

[8] T. Scott Miyakawa, *Protestants and Pioneers: Individualism and Conformity on the American Frontier* (Chicago: University of Chicago Press, 1964), pp. 234-235.

[9] E.g., see William W. Sweet, *Religion on the American Frontier,* vol. 1, *The Baptists* (New York: Henry Holt and Company, Inc., 1931).

[10] Henry F. May, *Protestant Churches and Industrial America* (New York: Harper & Row, Publishers, 1949), p. 14.

[11] Francis Wayland, *Elements of Moral Science* (Boston: Gould and Lincoln, 1852), pp. 200-201.

[12] Francis Wayland, *The Limitations of Human Responsibility* (Boston: Gould and Lincoln, 1838), pp. 136, 134. See Norman H. Maring, "The Individualism of Francis Wayland," in Hudson, ed., *Baptist Concepts of the Church,* pp. 135-169.

[13] In George S. Hendry, "The Theological Context of the Church Today," Edward J. Jurji, ed., *The Ecumenical Era in Church and Society* (New York: The Macmillan Co., 1959), p. 51.

[14] As quoted by Yahoshua Arieli, *Individualism and Nationalism in American Ideology* (Cambridge, Mass.: Harvard University Press, 1964), p. 240.

[15] "The Final Report of the STUDY COMMISSION ON DENOMINATIONAL STRUCTURE of the American Baptist Convention" (1972), p. 11.

[16] *Ibid.,* p. 100. The book referred to is by Norman H. Maring and Winthrop S. Hudson, *A Baptist Manual of Polity and Practice* (Valley Forge: Judson Press, 1963).

[17] *Foundations,* vol. 1, no. 1 (1958), p. 9.

PART I
ISSUES
DEFINED

1
Prolegomena to a Theology of Church Order

Baptist denominational life in America has been plagued by a basic schizophrenia, a schizophrenia rooted in contradictory understandings of the Christian faith and manifesting itself in antithetical methods of organization.

The one understanding of the Christian faith may be called a *"churchly" understanding.* It is rooted in the conviction that God's fundamental purpose in Christ was to create for himself a people, God's people, the body of Christ. In terms of this understanding, there are no solitary Christians. By definition Christians are related to one another. They belong together. They are part of one body. This understanding of the Christian faith found expression among Baptists in an ordered common life that is most frequently identified in terms of an association or convention type of organization.

The other understanding of the Christian faith is highly individualistic, and it may be called a *"nonchurchly" understanding.* It is rooted in the conviction that God's primary interest—indeed, exclusive interest—is in individual Christians. The Christian is thought of as a free man, the captain of his own soul, the master of his own fate, unbound and unfettered, under no necessity to ask by-your-leave of anyone. The consequence of this type of thinking, as someone has noted, is that every man's hat becomes his own church. Basically there is no church, only individual Christians. The organizational expressions of this type of thinking among Baptists have been societies, instruments fashioned by individuals to promote and forward particular ends.

The churchly understanding of the Christian faith is also undergirded by the conviction that Christians are dependent upon one another and need one another. They are dependent upon one another for what they know of Christ. Even the Scriptures have been preserved for them by the hands of others, and they need the nurture of a common life for their growth in grace and understanding. Recognizing their feebleness and frailty as finite, fallible men, they acknowledge that their understanding of the mind of Christ needs to be corrected by the insights of fellow Christians. An individual's knowledge is always partial, his experience limited, his perspective restricted; and these can only be broadened by the knowledge, experience, and differing perspectives of others, both living and dead. Moreover, personal prejudices and individual idiosyncrasies may color the thinking of even the best-intentioned Christian. Consequently, for this further reason, the views of any single Christian or group of Christians need to be checked by the views of others.

The nonchurchly understanding of the Christian faith exhibited a far greater confidence in the ability of the individual Christian to know and to do the will of God on his own. This self-confidence was partly the product of the natural human self-assertiveness that is ever ready to come to the fore when it is given any room for maneuver, and partly the product of the atomizing effect of the growing stress that was placed on the conversion experience as spelling out the length and the breadth of the Christian life. In America this self-confidence was reinforced by the sturdy and sometimes exuberant spirit of independence fostered by conditions of life in a new land and an expanding economy, and also by the highly individualistic philosophy that is most commonly associated with the names of John Locke, Thomas Jefferson, and Andrew Jackson. People increasingly thought of themselves as discrete, solitary individuals, existing in splendid isolation from their fellows, except in those instances when they freely and voluntarily chose to associate with others.

The implications for church life of these two differing points of view—the one acknowledging the frailty of the individual Christian and the other affirming the competency ("soul competency") of the individual Christian—were obvious and specific.

The churchly point of view thought of the church as God's creation. From a legal standpoint, to be sure, the church must be voluntary, for no one can or should be coerced by men (i.e., by the state) into being a Christian. But in a truer and deeper sense, the church is not voluntary. No one chooses to be a member of the church; he is made a member of the church. It is not his doing; it is God's doing. He is enticed, captivated, captured, mastered by

Christ, made one with Christ and one with all others whom Christ has chosen and called forth as God's people. Christians do not make the church; they are made the church.

The nonchurchly point of view has resulted in a completely antithetical understanding. The church becomes wholly voluntary. Christians make the church; it is their creation. Instead of being an organic body of persons who are indissolubly knit and linked together as one people, it is a voluntary society of individuals who freely unite for a specific purpose, most commonly defined as the public worship of God and the administration of God's ordinances—preaching, prayer, praise, baptism, the Lord's Supper, and "discipline."

The first view thinks of the local church as part of a larger whole—the whole church. It believes that all Christians, as members of one body, belong together. While they must of necessity assemble in particular local churches, they are not unrelated to other particular local churches. When there is opportunity and occasion to do so, their church must meet with other churches of like faith and order (commonly in a delegated or representative assembly) to carry out their common concerns as churches, and to subject themselves to correction and discipline at the hands of other churches.

The second opinion speaks in terms of "local autonomy." There is no church beyond the local church, other than the communion of saints in heaven. Particular local churches cannot meet in any representative or delegated assembly. The most that can be done is for messengers to meet for fellowship. Since the church is a voluntary society of individuals, the individuals who compose the church cannot be bound by the action of any delegates or representatives. This would abridge their independence. No one has any right to do anything for them nor to impose any requirement upon them. They remain free individuals, except insofar as they have united freely and voluntarily in a local society.

The first point of view is based upon a concern for unity. The second point of view is based upon an anarchical principle that breeds disunity, division, separation, fragmentation, and proliferation. The first is hesitant to make the opinion of any individual or group decisive, for he or they might be wrong. It is necessary to listen to others and to consider carefully the opinions they express. If there must be dissent and division, the division must be accepted regretfully, with a sense of repentance and with an acknowledgment that the judgment may be upon them rather than upon those with whom they differ. The second point of view feels little regret and repentance when the bond of unity is broken. The tendency is to be dogmatic and self-righteous in the expression of one's own views, and to rejoice in separation from those with whom one differs. The first point of view provides a basis both for a denominational ecclesiastical structure and for the maintenance of ecumenical relationships. The second point of view knows of no way by which a local church can reach out beyond itself.

Whatever their basic ideology, Christians have larger concerns than those represented by their own local church and their own local community. Those Baptists who adhered to the first or churchly point of view sought to deal with these concerns through an association or convention type of relationship. Those Baptists who became infected with the second or nonchurchly point of view sought to deal with these concerns through the formation of additional societies. What are the basic distinctions between these two types of organization?

The first distinction is in terms of *membership*. The association or convention is composed of churches. The members are churches. A church is admitted to membership in an association or convention, and it is then entitled to send delegates as its representatives to the meetings of the association or convention. The association or convention is thus an extension of the local church and shares in the life of the whole church in the same way that a local church does. A society, on the other hand, is composed of individuals. It has no necessary relationship to any church. Its members are individuals, most commonly those individuals who contribute to its funds. Most Baptist societies throughout the nineteenth century had only a financial require-ment for membership. Anyone who contributed was a member. A requirement that an individual belong to a Baptist church in order to be a member was ruled out on the ground that this would establish the society on an ecclesiastical base, and this was not to be permitted. This, of course, was an extreme position that had been propagated and popularized by Francis Wayland. Ordinarily a society could establish a number of membership requirements—financial, age, sex, denominational affiliation. The key distinction is that a society was composed of individuals, not churches.

The second distinction between an association or convention and a society is in terms of *purpose*. The association or convention, as an extension of the local church, is a multipurpose organiza-tion. It embraces the whole realm of the church's concern—

missions, publication, education, social issues, humanitarian need, men's work, women's work, youth work, church extension, theology, worship, "discipline," ordination, membership practices, pastoral placement, and anything else which may tend to the peace and prosperity of the church and the advancement of the gospel in the world. The society, on the other hand, is a single-purpose agency. It is concerned with a specific project, a single aim, a single goal.

It may be helpful, in pointing up the contrast between the association and the society, to illustrate, first of all, both the powers of an association and the scope of its concern. This may be done from the minutes of almost any association. The Pittsburgh Baptist Association, founded in 1839, may be regarded as typical. Its constitution, printed in the 1841 minutes, affirmed the rights of individual churches. All churches, it stated,

> have certain indefeasible rights, which are: receiving, dismissing, censuring, or expelling their own members; tolerating to improve or licensing to preach, such of their members as appear in their judgment to have gifts . . . , and silencing such of their members as may have been tolerated or licensed to preach, if the case may so require.

These are the rights vested in the local church—admission to membership, excommunication, and ordination.

But the association has its own powers. Not all churches, for example, may belong to the association. Only those churches may be admitted whose "faith and practice" is in harmony with the "doctrine and discipline" of the association. Furthermore, "if any church be suspected of departing from the doctrine or discipline of this association," after examination and trial, fellowship may be withdrawn. The Pittsburgh Association did not hesitate to use its power. The first session after its organization dealt with two issues of discipline. The first issue was resolved by the adoption of a rule that no church was to receive into its fellowship any "members that have been excluded by other churches, as we consider such conduct disorderly."

A second resolution dealt with the problem of licensing to preach, and it stated that churches of the association should "give no license to preach for a longer period than the next meeting of this association [three months], that the candidate may come under the examination of the ministers and messengers composing this body." In its circular letter or message to the churches, a third issue was raised which involved both doctrine and discipline. The letter dealt with the subject of Christian fellowship, and the churches were queried as to whether it was permissible in the light of Christian doctrine to maintain fellowship with those who held fellow Christians in a state of bondage. A year later, the letter having been discussed in the churches, the association adopted a resolution which stated that this association "can have no fellowship with those who are guilty of buying or selling their fellow men or who knowingly aid or abet this unrighteous traffic."

A few items will be sufficient to indicate the scope of the Pittsburgh Association's concern. At the initial meeting after its founding a major concern was to secure funds for the association to support "a missionary within our bounds." At the same meeting delegates were sent to a Baptist antislavery convention in New York City. In 1844 the association voted to support, with neighboring associations, Madison College at Uniontown, Pennsylvania. In 1856 the association was instrumental in establishing Western Seminary at McKeesport. In 1871 the association took the lead in founding Mt. Pleasant Institute. In 1862 the association began its Sunday school work. In 1864 the association established a Baptist bookstore in Pittsburgh. In 1874 the association began promoting the formation of women's missionary circles in the churches. In 1875 the association began the publication of a periodical, *The Baptist Witness*. In 1893 the association authorized the young people to proceed with the forming themselves into the B.Y.P.U. of the Pittsburgh Baptist Association. In 1904 the association took over the work and the funds of the Church Aid and Extension Society.

The singleness of aim of the society method of organization, in contrast to the multipurpose associational structure, may be illustrated by a mere listing of societies—the American Bible Society, the American Tract Society, the American Education Society, the American Peace Society, the American Temperance Society, the American Antislavery Society, the American Antidueling Society, the American Society for the Aid of Females Who Have Deviated from the Paths of Virtue, the American Seamen's Friend Society, the American Baptist Foreign Mission Society, the American Baptist Home Mission Society, the American Baptist Publication Society, the American Baptist Education Society, the American Baptist Historical Society, the Chicago Baptist City Mission Society, the Anti-Saloon League, the Women's Christian Temperance Union. The list is endless. Each society is formed for a specific purpose. This is indispensable from the point of view of the proponents of the society type of organization. As a church, defined in terms of a voluntary society, cannot coerce its members by uniting them with other churches, so societies other than a local church must be limited to a single purpose in order to preserve the individual member's liberty and freedom of choice. An individual Christian may be interested in the distribution of Bibles but opposed to foreign missions; he may be strong for temperance but view dueling with equanimity; he may be in favor of promoting Sunday schools but indifferent to other educational needs; he may be eager to forward the cause of peace but an ardent defender of the institution of slavery. The single-purpose society is designed to safeguard the freedom of the individual Christian by avoiding such conflicting interests and concerns. This is the second marked contrast between an association or convention structure and a society structure of denominational organization.

In addition to making certain that an individual Christian shall remain totally free and uncoerced by limiting membership to individuals and by restricting the purpose to a single project, the society method of organization had two distinct advantages. The society method permitted both quick action and concerted action. As soon as a need emerged, those who recognized the need did not have to wait until a whole church or association could be persuaded to act. A few interested individuals could form a society, get on with the job, and then proceed to enlist further support. Moreover, they could concentrate their energies on this single task without being held back or diverted by other concerns.

While the society procedure had great utility as an emergency and interim method of meeting a specific need, it had very serious disadvantages as a structure for denominational organization. First, it ruled out the possibility of overall planning. A multiplicity of independent societies, each pursuing its own specific concern, provided no opportunity to establish priorities and to develop a coherent and carefully thought-out denominational strategy. Second, as a result of the society pattern of organization the churches were plagued with a multiplicity of financial appeals. This was not only bothersome to the churches, but also the necessity for each society to send agents into the field to collect funds was grossly inefficient and expensive. Third, the society method of organization lent itself to the control of denominational enterprises by a small clique. An individual in Ashtabula, Ohio, who contributed ten dollars and thus became a member of a society, could not be expected to attend the annual meeting in

Philadelphia, New York, or Boston. His stake in the society was not large enough to warrant the trip. If he could afford to make the trip, he could not afford to do so more than once or twice. Even local societies did not draw any large number of members to their annual meetings, for the only business was the routine task of electing members to the board of the society.[1] Furthermore, the average individual had neither the time nor the energy to participate in all the societies to which he may have contributed. As a result of these factors, the boards of the societies tended to become self-perpetuating and essentially irresponsible (i.e., responsible only to themselves).

The churches, in the end, refused to put up with such a confused, anarchical, and irresponsible system of denominational organization. The national societies were induced to schedule simultaneous annual meetings in the same city so that more members might attend. Provision was made for churches as well as individuals to be members. Efforts were made to coordinate appeals for funds. Informal consultations sought to develop priorities and a common strategy. None of this was very effective, and no real degree of order was introduced until the American (Northern) Baptist Convention was organized in 1907 with the ultimate effect of reducing the societies to the status of boards of the convention. The state conventions underwent a similar evolution, and most of the city mission societies were absorbed by local associations.

The most crucial, although not the most immediate and obvious disadvantage of the society structure was the fact that it tended to destroy any idea of the church's having a corporate life extending beyond the local congregation.[2] The churches were unable either to speak or to act as a denomination, and this reduced their influence and effectiveness. The society structure also tended to eliminate among church members any sense of belonging to a larger whole. Churches were simply regarded as isolated units with some members who might chance to be involved in cooperative activities that were quite independent of their local church. Such a structure was ill-designed to foster *esprit de corps*. In such a situation there was an inevitable tendency for churches to drift in contradictory directions, and for the denomination to suffer disunity and division.

The society structure was ultimately abandoned and the practice of the denomination was reformed to get rid of the manifest disorder, anarchy, inefficiency, and ineffectiveness it entailed. But the great tragedy has been that the ideological, or rather theological, problem was never faced. The shibboleths of the architects of the society system—the most prominent being the twin doctrines of "soul competency" and "local autonomy"— linger on to create confusion, introduce dissension, inhibit action, and prevent any intelligent statement of the theological under-girding of denominational life from being formulated. This final consequence, the lack of any intelligible theology of church order, has been the most serious. It has meant that the denomination has had to stumble into administrative reforms and reorganization on an *ad hoc* basis without the benefit of any theological guidelines to help determine the decisions that have been made. Since crucial theological points often involve subtle and complex ecclesiastical construction, the denomination has been denied what it so desperately needs if it is to be faithful to its calling in Christ.

Perhaps the best way to approach the question of what is involved in the task of ecclesiastical construction is to review some of the facets of early Baptist church life, in order to note the sensitive points at which they were most careful in fashioning a structure for denominational life.[3] They were aware of opposite perils at several points, and they sought to pursue a "middle way" between them. This emphasis upon a "middle way" was the basic theme of the so-called Non-Separatist Independents from whom the early Baptists in America inherited both the principles and structures of their church life. The *Apologetical Narration* of the Dissenting Brethren (Thomas Goodwin, Philip Nye, William Bridge, Jeremiah Burroughes, and William Greenhill) in the Westminster Assembly makes this point clear:

> We believe the truth to lie and consist in a middle way betwixt that which is falsely charged upon us, Brownism [a hyperseparatism], and that which is the contention of these times, the authoritative presbyterial government in all the subordinations and proceedings of it.

It was made clear again a short time later in Thomas Goodwin's and Philip Nye's preface to John Cotton's treatise on church government, *The Keys of the Kingdom of Heaven*. We are "neither afraid nor ashamed," wrote Goodwin and Nye, "to make profession (in the midst of all the high waves on both sides dashing on us)" of "that very middle way . . . between that which is called Brownism and the Presbyterial government as it is practiced." This "middle way" was described and explicated in dozens of pamphlets, but it found its most concise and orderly statement in the Platform of Government which was appended to the Savoy Declaration and then incorporated by the Baptists in their London or Philadelphia Confession as their Article on the Church, and was then further explicated in Baptist treatises of church discipline.[4]

The Non-Separatists, who fashioned the principles and practice to which the major group of Baptists adhered, were accused of being Brownists. This they denied. "We had the fatal miscarriages and shipwrecks of the Separation (whom you call Brownists) to forewarn us of those rocks and shelves they ran upon, which did put us upon an inquiry into the principles that might be the cause of their divisions." These principles which permitted contention, strife, and division to develop, the Non-Separatists were determined to avoid. But they were equally determined to avoid the tyranny of "authoritative presbyterial government in all the subordinations and proceedings of it."

The most important Scylla and Charybdis that they had to navigate was between the respective powers of local congregations and of synods or associations.[5] They were charged with being Independents, but it was a label they repudiated, insisting that they were not independent of God, of Christ, of the Bible, or of one another. Their "middle way" was put tersely in the *Apologetical Narration.* They claimed no "independent power in every congregation" so that there is no need "to give an account or be subject to . . . others." They claimed only "a full and entire power complete" in each congregation "until" a congregation "should be challenged to err grossly." Then it may be called to account. What they did reject was the notion that "the combination of elders of many churches should be the first complete and entire seat of church power over each congregation."

As sons of the Reformation and students of Scripture, the Non-Separatists rejected any sacerdotal concept of the church. The church was not dependent for its existence upon any special sacerdotal powers conveyed in holy orders (ordination). In Christ all special priestly powers had been abolished, and all Christians were equally priests or equally laymen. Thus, the Non-Separatists agreed with Luther, who had said that any company of Christians in a wilderness was fully equipped to minister Christ and had no need to derive authority from anywhere, other than from Christ, to choose their own officers, to administer baptism and the Lord's Supper, and to become fully a church. On the other hand, such a company of Christians was not unrelated to other Christians, and the Non-Separatists were emphatic in their insistence that no local company of Christians should heedlessly disregard the bonds which bound them to other Christians.

In legal terms the question at issue was the location of initial jurisdiction in the church. The question of initial jurisdiction had its focus in the three key points of church power—admission to church membership, excommunication, and ordination. The first point, admission to membership, was not in debate. It was obvious that the local congregation was in the best position to judge a person's qualifications for membership. The second and third points were the controversial ones. The Non-Separatists, many of whom had been ejected from their pulpits, had good reason to be aware that faithful Christians had been intimidated and congregations coerced into unwarranted practices by excommunications threatened and imposed by distant courts. This, they contended, was a violation of the fundamental power of a congregation, and furthermore it was unjust. As any man charged with a civil offense had the right to trial by a jury of his peers in his own community, so a man threatened by the much more terrible penalty of having his soul delivered to Satan should have the right to be tried by those who knew him best, the members of his own congregation. The third point at which the issue of jurisdiction was raised was in connection with the power of ordination. The Non-Separatists had also had the experience of having ungodly or unworthy ministers thrust upon unwilling congregations. To guard against this possibility, it was insisted that the essence of the outward calling of a minister resides in the consent of the congregation. The fundamental contention of the Non-Separatists with regard to jurisdiction was that church power, defined in terms of the power to admit to membership, to excommunicate, and to ordain, belonged to the local congregation and not to any superior judicatory.

Having avoided the Scylla of authoritative presbyterial government, the Non-Separatists were equally concerned to escape the Charybdis of separatism. They had no desire to see the bond of unity shattered and divisions multiplied by wayward congregations. Congregations could be perverse and disorderly in their proceedings and could become unfaithful to their calling, but they should not be permitted to go their heedless way unwarned and unadmonished. Provision should be made to preserve the unity of the brethren in the bond of peace. "Because these particular congregations, both elders and people," wrote Goodwin and Nye, "may disagree and miscarry and abuse this power committed to them," there is necessity for

> an association or communion of churches sending their elders and messengers into a synod . . . unto whom Christ hath . . . committed a due and just measure of power . . . and furnished them not only with ability to give counsel and advice, but further . . . with a ministerial power and authority to determine, declare, and enjoin such things as may tend to the reducing [of] such congregations to right order and peace.[6]

The association or synod, while having no primary jurisdiction and unable to initiate proceedings, is a body to which appeal can be made when things have gone amiss. Congregations retain full power until they abuse it and "err grossly." Actually this is a slight misstatement, for a congregation retains its powers even when it errs grossly. What occurs is that the power of the association becomes operative. This was a point of some confusion to early Baptists in America, and an *Essay on the Power and Duty of an Association of Churches* was drafted to clarify the point. An association may determine (decide) the matter at issue and may declare and decree the observation of its determination, but it may not "impose" its determination upon the churches. The determination must be voluntarily accepted and implemented, for the power involved in implementation still belongs to the churches. If a church, however, should fail to heed the decision of the association, the offending church may then be excluded from the association. "In the capacity of a congregational church dealing with her own members, an association . . . may exclude and withdraw from defective and unsound and disorderly churches." Thus, a church is not free to do as it wishes and still remain part of the larger body.

The discussion thus far has pointed to the fact that these architects of a "middle way" between complete "separatism" and "authoritative presbyterial government" had been taught by their experience and by their understanding of the Christian faith that power may be abused. While they were convinced that Christians were a single people and belonged together, and that institutional expression must be given to this fact, they were equally convinced that any concentration of power in a centralized authority would lend itself to tyrannical abuse. On the other hand, they were also aware that unchecked power in the hands of local congregations could lead to equal (although less threatening) abuse and waywardness. Their "middle way" was the dispersal, distribution, or separation of powers so characteristic of those who had learned to suspect and fear the deceit which forever lurks within the human heart.

The Non-Separatists and their Baptist heirs also sought to pursue a "middle way" within the local congregation. All Protestants were clear in their understanding that the pastoral office was an office and not a separate order in the church. Ordination did not confer any unique, indelible character to the person ordained. It simply authorized or commissioned him to assume certain responsibilities on behalf of other members of the church. There was a tendency among some, however, to regard this as a rather complete delegation of power; and there was a tendency among others to regard it as no real delegation of authority at all, the pastoral office being little more than a perfunctory designation to perform routine tasks. Thomas Goodwin and Philip Nye stated the issue very clearly. "In those former darker times," they wrote, "this golden ball" of church power "was thrown up by the clergy to run for among themselves." This independent power of the clergy the Presbyterians had not been willing fully to surrender, for their clergy gained their status not from the local church in which they served but from a regional presbytery or synod to which they belonged. And, by virtue of the power derived therefrom, a Presbyterian clergyman was largely able to command and rule the body of the church without restraint. A second "unhappiness" of "these latter times" has been for "knowing saints" to "err on the other extreme" by claiming for the congregation "the whole power" and by insisting "that the elders set over them did but exercise that power for them which was properly" the congregation's, and "which Christ . . . originally estated in the people only." This was the error of the Brownists, who "in effect put the chief (if not the whole) of the rule and government in the hands of the people and drown the elders' votes (who are but few) in the major part of theirs." The Presbyterian error led to clericalism; the Brownist error led to self-assertive willfulness on the part of an ignorant, uninformed, and uninstructed congregation.

The Brownist error was rooted in a misunderstanding of the purpose of the pastoral office. One of the major responsibilities of the pastor was to instruct and admonish the members of the congregation. He was chosen for the pastoral office because of his sensitivity, discernment, judgment, and maturity, and because he was learned (and given the opportunity to become learned) in the Scriptures and their interpretation. One man's opinion was not as good as another man's opinion in the life of the church. The gospel was to be taken seriously, and this required the pastor's sensitivity, discernment, judgment, maturity, and knowledge. The pastor, however, could not be trusted to act independently of the congregation. With all his gifts, he was subject to common human frailty and needed to be checked by the congregation. The pastor must be able to persuade and convince the congregation. What was necessary, in the words of Goodwin and Nye, was "a suitable and due-proportioned distribution and dispersion of power" between pastor and people, with "the whole" being given "to neither part."

What the Non-Separatists proposed was a "mixed government," embracing elements of monarchy, aristocracy, and democracy. The monarchical element was represented by the kingship of Christ. Christ was the king and lawgiver. No church had any legislative authority. The will of the people was never to prevail. Their task was to discover ("determine" was the word they used) the will of Christ and to do it. The aristocratic element was represented by the elders ("a speaking aristocracy"), and the democratic element by the congregation ("a silent democracy"). Any action required the concurrence of both elders and people. The analogy here is not really to a bicameral legislature with action requiring the assent of both houses, but more properly to a judge and jury. The law was given, the judge instructed the jury, the jury made the determination, and the judge pronounced the sentence. Theoretically, in this instance, the judge would possess the power of veto, for his concurrence with the verdict of the jury was necessary.

While this cumbersome procedure did not long persist, its intent was clear. The pastor was to be taken seriously and due deference given to his opinion, if the gospel were to be taken seriously. Only an informed and instructed congregation could be trusted as a delicate and sensitive instrument to determine God's will for his people. Various other expedients were devised by Baptists to safeguard the role of the pastor in the congregation. The members of the churches were constantly admonished in the various disciplines or manuals about the "obedience" they owed to him "in the Lord," and care was taken to emphasize his "presidential authority" in the life of the church.

A third "middle way" was between the "inclusiveness" of the parish church and the "exclusive sectarianism" of Brownist separatism. The concept of the church as a "mixed multitude," embracing everyone living within the bounds of a geographical parish, was rejected. The notion of a "pure" church, with its corollary that any church suffering any taint of impurity was a synagogue of Satan, was also rejected. It seemed obvious to those who sought this "middle way" that a church should be composed of believers (for the Baptists, believers who had been baptized on the professon of their faith). On the other hand, the Non-Separatists and their heirs among the Baptists had few illusions as to the possibility of achieving a "pure" church. Their judgments at the door of the church had to be judgments of charity and could result only in approximation of a "pure" church, for God alone knows those who are truly his people. "The purest churches under heaven are subject to mixture and error," the Baptists acknowledged. Furthermore, they were well aware of their own fallibility. "We confess that we know but in part, and that we are ignorant of many things which we desire and seek to know; and if any shall do us that friendly part to show us from the word of God that we see not, we shall have cause to be thankful to God and them." With this dual admission, they were no more prepared than the Non-Separatists to deny the name of Christian to all who differed from them. Thus, while they had to be faithful to the light they had received and to practice what they had been led to profess, they still found it possible in good conscience to maintain fellowship in varying ways with those who differed from them and to work together in common tasks.

This two-fold review of past history—first, of the ideas and influences which sharply modified Baptist church life in the nineteenth century, and, second, of the concerns which shaped several facets of early Baptist ecclesiology—can serve only as prolegomena to the task of fashioning an adequate theology of church order. They call attention to some basic theological principles, but the more important contribution is to point to the interplay of theological and pragmatic considerations in all ecclesiastical construction. Church order should express and not violate or distort fundamental theological convictions, but the specific forms and structures that are devised must always take into account changing circumstance and shifting needs. Consequently, for a living church, the outward forms and structures through which it seeks to express its inward life can never remain static, but must be subject to constant review.

NOTES

[1] Dodges occasionally were employed to reduce the possibility of even this minimal participation. The Baptist Education Society of the State of New York

organized a subsidiary society, the Society of Friends and Alumni, to collect contributions for the parent society, while the Baptist Theological Union of Illinois solicited funds through the Northwest Baptist Education Society. This procedure, of course, kept contributors from becoming members of the parent society and thus prevented them from having even a limited voice in its affairs through the election of board members.

[2] The society philosophy, of course, tended to destroy even the idea of the local church as a corporate body. It viewed the local church as a collection of individuals who had voluntarily affiliated themselves for a common purpose rather than as a body bound together in a common life.

[3] Two historical points should be made in connection with the following discussion:

First, there were two currents of Baptist life, that represented by the Particular or Calvinistic Baptists and that represented by the General or Arminian Baptists. In terms of our present concern the latter stream may be disregarded for two reasons. The mainstream of American Baptist life stems from the Particular Baptist current, modified to be sure by the influence of the New England "Separates," who were also Calvinistic in theology. Furthermore, the Arminian Baptists, both in their earlier form as General Baptists and in their later Wesleyan form as Free Will Baptists, developed a highly centralized denominational life that was quite different from the pattern of denominational life developed by the Particular Baptists. Consequently, the issues raised by their form of organization are not directly relevant to the problems of the major Baptist groups in America, and the introduction of these issues would serve to confuse rather than to clarify our problems.

Second, the rationale for the ecclesiastical structures adopted by the Particular Baptists frequently can be understood only by referring to the writings and documents of the Non-Separatist Independents. This is not an unreasonable procedure for several reasons: (1) The Particular Baptists had their origin in Henry Jacob's Non-Separatist Independent congregation. (2) The point at issue in their separation from the Jacob congregation was the question of baptism, not theology in general nor any other issues of church order. (3) When the Particular Baptists adopted their Confession of Faith (the London Confession of 1677 in England and the Philadelphia Confession in America), they incorporated in it, as their article on "The Church," the Platform of Government which the Non-Separatist Independent group had appended to their Savoy Declaration of Faith. While the Particular Baptists made minor changes in the Savoy Declaration recension of the Westminster Confession of Faith (substituting, for example, the hyper-Calvinist triple covenant for the double covenant), the fundamental distinction between the two groups remained at the point of baptism. (4) For a century and a half the Particular Baptists constantly identified themselves with the Non-Separatist understanding of the church and church order by referring the reader of Particular Baptist documents to such prominent Non-Separatist divines as John Owen and Thomas Goodwin for further explication of their position. There would seem to be no reason not to take the Particular Baptists at their word and to consult the Non-Separatist writings for this further explication. Nor is it surprising that the Particular Baptists did not produce extended expositions of their position on the point of church order. This had been hammered out in an earlier controversy. The controversy had become quiescent; the position was well established and could largely be taken for granted by the Particular Baptists. Furthermore, adequate expositions were available, as they took care to point out. Thus, when the Particular Baptists in their confessions of faith, disciplines, and other documents reproduced (even verbally) the pattern of church order fashioned by the Non-Separatist Independents, we may assume that they retained this pattern for the reasons which caused it to be fashioned in the first place and with which they were familiar.

[4] The *Apologetical Narration* has recently been reprinted with an introduction by

Robert S. Paul. It is also reproduced in William Haller, *Tracts on Liberty*. The Preface to Cotton's *Keys of the Kingdom of Heaven* may be found in A. S. P. Woodhouse, *Puritanism and Liberty*. The Savoy Declaration and Platform of Government is in Williston Walker, *Creeds and Platforms of Congregationalism*. This latter volume also contains the Cambridge Platform, another formulation of the middle way which is in basic harmony with early Baptist practice but to which the early Baptists were not directly indebted. Excerpts from some of the Baptist documents are reprinted in *Foundations*, vol. 4, no. 1 (Oct., 1961), pp. 332-339.

[5] Synod was the common early term; association later replaced it in the common usage of Congregationalists and Baptists.

[6] The Discipline of 1743, which the Philadelphia Baptist Association drafted and appended to its Confession of Faith, used almost identical words in speaking of the role of the association: "Such messengers and delegates . . . may declare and determine the mind of the Holy Ghost revealed in Scripture concerning things in difference, and may decree the observation of things that are true and necessary."

2
The Associational Principle Among Baptists

We are always tempted to interpret the past in the light of the present. For several generations Baptists have been arch-individualists. They have contended that the local church exists in complete and splendid isolation, and they have insisted that their associational bodies have no real powers. While Baptists have never made their practice square completely with their theory during these years, by and large this is what they have believed. In view of this prevailing mind set, it is not surprising that the whole of Baptist history should have been interpreted from this relatively modern point of view. The result has been that Baptists have been left without any guiding principles or foundational supports for their organized denominational life and have been largely inhibited by this fact from taking constructive action to meet the exigencies of changing conditions. The only thing that could be done was to improvise—usually with a guilty conscience—and this, on the whole, has served only to create further anomalies. If this unhappy situation is to be brought to an end, it is important for us to understand the associational principle as it was operative among the early Baptists.

I

It has been suggested that "organized connectional or denominational life among American Baptists developed quite slowly" and that this was to be "expected in the case of churches which emphasized their own independency."[1] Actually, this statement is wrong on both counts. Organized denominational life among American Baptists did not develop slowly, nor is there any real reason to expect that it should have developed slowly.

The major Baptist bodies in the United States all stem from the Philadelphia Baptist Association. It is true that the Philadelphia Baptist Association was not organized until 1707, a full century after the first settlement was established at Jamestown in Virginia. But to suggest that this represents a late development among Baptists would be to assume that, as soon as John Rolfe married Pocahontas, Baptists began to spring up everywhere in the American colonies. It should be remembered that William Penn did not arrive in Pennsylvania with his first settlers until 1682, and that the first Baptist church in the Middle Colonies was not formed until 1686.* Within the next few years three other churches were formed, and these four churches met together for informal quarterly meetings. As soon as there was one additional church, the Philadelphia Baptist Association was organized.

It was much the same story with regard to the other Associations. When Oliver Hart arrived in South Carolina from Philadelphia to form the Charleston Association (1751), there were still only four Baptist churches in the state. The Sandy Creek Association in North Carolina and Virginia was formed in 1758 within three years from the time Shubal Stearns had begun to gather Baptist churches in the area. Other Associations in North Carolina, Virginia, Pennsylvania, Connecticut, and Vermont were formed with equal dispatch. Only in eastern Massachusetts, among Separate Congregationalists turned Baptists, was there any marked delay. As Massachusetts Congregationalists they had not been accustomed to having connectional bodies, and so it was not until the Philadelphia Association took the initiative that the Warren Association was formed in 1767.

II

The major difficulty in interpreting the early history of the Baptists has been a misunderstanding of what they meant by the emphasis upon the "independence" of "particular churches." It certainly was not regarded by them as a barrier to union among the churches.

---

*The earliest Baptist churches, of course, were in Rhode Island. With the exception of the Newport church and two Seventh Day Baptist churches, these were General Six Principle Baptist churches. To them belongs the honor of forming the earliest Association. In 1670 they united in a yearly meeting, composed of elders and messengers, for "setting in order the things that were wanting" and for resolving "any difficulties that might arise." This group never entered the mainstream of American Baptist life, although several of its churches were to withdraw and join the Warren Association under the influence of men from Philadelphia. This group reached the peak of its strength in 1729 and slowly dwindled thereafter. By 1955 only five churches, with 324 members, remained.

In seventeenth-century England, those who advocated a congregational form of church government were called quite indiscriminately "Independents." It was not a name which they chose for themselves; it was a name given to them by their opponents. They ultimately became resigned to being known as Independents, but only under protest. For they asserted that they were not independent of God, of Christ, of the Bible, or of one another. The extent of their "independence" was their assertion that a particular church, properly organized, has all the necessary means of grace appointed by Christ and has no need to derive any further authority from outside its own life. Its ministry does not derive its authority from a bishop or a presbytery, but from the inward call of Christ confirmed and acknowledged by the outward call of the congregation. Nor is the power of the church any less complete in matters of discipline. It is the custodian of the censures of the church—the keys to the kingdom—and it alone can excommunicate and deliver a soul to Satan.

The Independents had learned, with good reason, to be fearful of ecclesiastical tyranny. They had had experience of unwanted and ungodly ministers being intruded upon congregations, and they were asserting that there can be no ministry in a church without the congregation's calling. They had also had experience of Christians being coerced into what they regarded as unwarranted and ungodly practices by the power of excommunication wielded by bishops and synods, and they were insisting that if any one were to be subjected to this terrible penalty it must be done by those who knew him best, by his own fellow believers in his own congregation.

In terms of the Independents' analysis, a particular church is not just a fraction of the Catholic Church; it *is* the Catholic Church. Where a church possesses the Scriptures, the preaching of the Word, the declaration of the Word in baptism and the Lord's Supper, and properly constituted discipline and government, it is equipped to minister Christ in the place where it is set, and no body can be more fully or more truly the Church. This is the mark of its catholicity—the fullness of its life in making Christ manifest to the world.

But this did not mean that a truly constituted church could exist in isolation from other churches. While it is fully the Church, it is but one manifestation of the whole Church of God, and it must seek to maintain fellowship with other churches. The customary pattern was for representatives from the churches to meet together to bear witness to their common unity in Christ, to increase their love and communion with one another, to share their gifts in mutual edification, to deal with their common concerns, to provide brotherly counsel, and to preserve peace and unity among the churches. While such bodies composed of representatives from the churches had no "church power" over the churches (i.e., they could neither ordain nor excommunicate), the representatives when gathered together did constitute a body that had "lawful right" to "act in the name of Christ" and to order its own common life.

With the exception of the Sandy Creek Association, which drew its pattern from late Connecticut Congregationalism and apparently assumed both the powers of ordination and excommunication, the early Baptist Associations represent the traditional Independent point of view which has been described. Since the Philadelphia Association was the earliest of the Associations and since the others were formed on the Philadelphia plan, the Philadelphia Association may be regarded as more or less normative and may serve as a case study of the associational pattern among Baptists.

III

The general doctrinal position of the Philadelphia Association with regard to the Church and the churches is set forth in its Confession of Faith. "The Catholic or Universal Church . . . ," it states, "consists of the whole number of the elect that have been, are, or shall be gathered into one under Christ, the head thereof." The assembling of the whole Church must inevitably await the Last Judgment, but in the meantime those who are at present upon the earth and who have been given to Christ by his Father and called by Christ through the ministry of his Word are to "walk before him in all the ways of obedience which he prescribeth." They are commanded specifically "to walk together in particular societies or churches for their mutual edification and the due performance of that public worship which he requireth of them." Furthermore, "being united to one another in love," they "are obliged to the performance of such duties, public and private, in an orderly way, as do conduce to their mutual good both in the inward and outward man." Lastly, "to each of these churches, thus gathered according to his mind declared in his Word," Christ "hath given all that power and authority which is any way needful for their carrying on that order in worship and discipline which he hath instituted for them to observe, with commands and rules for the due and right exerting and executing of that power."

While considerations of time and space and number dictated the necessity for believers to be gathered into particular churches and while these particular churches were endowed with all the authority necessary fully to minister Christ in the place where they were set, nevertheless they were not unrelated to one another. "As each church and all the members of it are bound to pray continually for the good and prosperity of all the churches of Christ," the Confession asserts, ". . . so the churches, when planted by the providence of God so as they may enjoy opportunity and advantage for it, ought to hold communion amongst themselves for their peace, increase of love, and mutual edification."

The specific "duties" through which the "communion of churches" was to be expressed was spelled out by the Discipline of 1743.* One church, for example, that "hath plenty of gifts," i.e., ministerial gifts, "ought, if possible, to supply another that lacketh." Also there should be a "mutual giving and receiving" in the "recommendation or dismission of members from one church to another as occasion may require." Furthermore, "by virtue of such communion, the members of one church may . . . partake at the Lord's Table with a sister church." But there are other occasions when it is necessary to take counsel together and to cooperate in joint endeavors for the benefit of all. For these purposes, "it is expedient that particular churches . . . , when they are planted by the providence of God so as they may have opportunity and advantage so to do, should by their mutual agreement appoint proper times and places to meet by their respective messengers or delegates to consider of such things as may be for the common benefit of all such churches, for their peace, prosperity, and mutual edification, and what may be for the furtherance of the gospel and the interest of Christ in the world."

---

*Benjamin Griffith, in his preface to the Discipline of 1743, notes that in drafting the Discipline he had consulted the writings of John Owen and Thomas Goodwin; and the Discipline of 1798 refers the reader to the writings of these same men and to those of Thomas Hooker for further explication of the points discussed. Elias Keach's *The Glory and Ornament of a True Gospel-constituted Church* (1697), which was also used in drafting the Discipline of 1743, adds William Ames and Isaac Chauncey to the list of divines whose writings are to be consulted. These names alone should be sufficient to indicate the context within which the activities of the Philadelphia Association must be understood, for they all were major spokesmen for the group which Perry Miller has identified as non-separatist Independents.

It is sometimes suggested that Baptist churches, being wholly independent bodies, cannot delegate authority to any other body to act in their behalf, and that the only way that Baptists can get anything done cooperatively is for individual members of churches to form voluntary societies for specific purposes, making sure that these voluntary societies have no "ecclesiastical" basis. Such a contention, however, cannot be substantiated by an appeal to either early Baptist theory or practice. While it is true that Baptists have formed voluntary societies, there is nothing distinctively Baptist about such a procedure. Christians of all denominations, including Roman Catholics, have also done so. The traditional Baptist pattern and the continuing practice has been for churches to cooperate and to express their communion with one another by forming Associations. The point to emphasize is that these Associations were not Associations of individuals but Associations of *churches*. They were composed of delegates or representatives who were designated and authorized, as the Plan of the Warren Association put it, to act on behalf of the churches.

The Philadelphia Association was typical in this respect. In 1762, in a communication to the Board of Ministers in London, the Association gives as its official title "The Association of Particular Baptist Churches annually held at Philadelphia." Among Southern Baptists in recent years there has been a tendency to insist upon the term "messenger" instead of "delegate" to designate members of Baptist assemblies, on the supposition that "delegate" means "representative" and that Baptist churches cannot be "represented." Actually the three words have always been used as synonomous and interchangeable terms. Throughout the Minutes of the Philadelphia Association, for example, the members of the Association constantly refer to themselves as "your representatives" and "your delegates," and they usually address their communications to "the congregations we represent."

IV

The nature, function, and scope of an Association of Churches, acting in behalf of the churches, can best be seen in terms of the actual activities carried on by the Philadelphia Association.

One of the major purposes of the Association was to provide mutual edification. The four original churches in the Middle Colonies, prior to the formation of the Association, had been accustomed to meet together at stated periods for preaching and the observance of the Lord's Supper, and this practice was continued as a central feature of associational life. The accepted pattern was to have a sermon on Saturday afternoon when the Association convened, to have another sermon the following morning, a third sermon followed by the Lord's Supper in the afternoon, and a concluding sermon on Monday morning. For the edification of those not present, a Circular Letter or Pastoral Address, containing "suitable exhortations," was sent out to be read to the congregations of the member churches. The subject matter of the letter varied. It might contain encouragements to greater unity, zeal, and faithfulness; or it might discuss points of doctrine, the duties of church members, the nature of the pastoral office, or the necessity for missionary endeavor.

A second major preoccupation of the Association was the problem of providing a suitable and regular ministry for the churches. This involved the development of procedures for the recruitment, education, ordination, and placement of ministers, as well as the establishment of strict regulations to control the frequently troublesome activities of itinerant preachers. Since there was a chronic shortage of ministers, the "destitute" churches were denied the comfort of the ordinances, including preaching. They might suffer one of their members to exhibit his "gifts" on trial for a time, but, except for this slight concession, these churches were restricted in their worship to singing, praying, and reading from the Bible. Later, it was suggested that one of their number might also read from "some sound, profitable, approved sermon books."[2]

In this situation, pastorless churches were strongly tempted to welcome almost any itinerant who might appear, claiming to be a Baptist preacher. To guard against this danger, it was agreed at the first meeting of the Association in 1707 that no stranger "shall be allowed to preach among the associated churches, except he produce credentials of his being in communion with his church and of his having been called and licensed to preach."[3] A few years later, this regulation was further tightened by requiring that the Association itself examine and certify "all gifted brethren and ministers that come in here from other places . . . , we have found the evil of neglecting a true and previous scrutiny in those affairs."[4]

Initially the churches were primarily dependent upon ministers who came to them from abroad, but the Association was constantly urging the churches to seek out prospective ministers among their own members, and steps were taken to provide these promising young men with the necessary education for their task. Illustrative of the early procedure is the minute of 1722 which requested the churches "to make inquiry among themselves, if they have any young persons hopeful for the ministry and inclinable for learning; and if they have, to give notice of it to Mr. Abel Morgan . . . that he might recommend such to the academy on Mr. Hollis, his account." The Hollis account was a fund provided by Thomas Hollis, a London merchant, and it served as the nucleus of the educational fund of the Association, out of which grants were made to permit candidates for the ministry to pursue their studies. It was not until 1756 that the churches were numerous enough and strong enough for the Association to attempt to establish an academy of its own. Eight years later, in 1764, the Philadelphia Association commissioned James Manning to found the College of Rhode Island so that Baptists might have a collegiate institution of their own for the training of ministers. The educational fund to aid individual students was continued, a new academy was set up under the direction of Samuel Jones at Lower Dublin, and a form of in-service training was provided by establishment of a circulating library.[5]

A third concern of the Association was to supply the churches with needed printed materials, and to this end it engaged in considerable publishing activity. These materials were designed to meet the varied needs of the churches, and they included the Confession of Faith, the Treatise of Discipline, a catechism for the instruction of children, and a hymnal.* The Circular Letter, which was an extended discussion of a single topic, was first printed as a separate item, and then as a part of the Minutes. In addition to these standard materials, the Association published a treatise on baptism in 1746, a treatise on apologetics in 1749, a treatise on family worship in 1769, a treatise on the parables by Benjamin

* The Confession and the Treatise of Discipline were printed for the Association by Benjamin Franklin in 1743. They were reprinted in 1765, and there were apparently other editions. The Minutes of 1724 refer to the Confession of Faith "owned by us," and three years later the reference is to "our Confession of Faith" in "our last edition." A previous Discipline may have been printed, for the Minutes of 1728 and 1735 refer to "our Treatise of Discipline," and in 1737 the page numbers are cited. The most frequently printed item was the Catechism. According to the Minutes, a reprinting of the Catechism was authorized in 1738, and new editions are noted in 1747, 1761, and 1779. The hymnal is noted in the minutes of 1788. Two other books listed for sale by the Association were Stennett's Sermons and Edwards' Customs of Primitive Churches. The Minutes of 1774 inform us, however, that the latter volume must not be regarded as reflecting the views of the Association, since the author had neglected to submit it to the Association for correction and approval.

Keach in 1771, an abridgment of Gill's *Exposition of the Bible* in 1787, a treatise on the education of children in 1795, and the first two volumes of Morgan Edwards' history of the Baptists in the various colonies in 1770 and 1792. The status of some other volumes is not clear, whether they were published by the Association or merely sold by the Association. Still other volumes, published and sold independently, were warmly recommended.

A fourth major area in which the Association acted in behalf of the churches was in the field of missions. It is occasionally suggested that the Philadelphia Association did not begin missionary activity until 1755 when the Minutes note that two of the ministering brethren were sent to North Carolina at Association expense. Actually Virginia had been repeatedly visited by Philadelphia missionaries since 1745,[6] and a public fund was created by the Association in 1750, presumably for their support. It is probable that this type of missionary activity was carried on from the very beginning of the Association, and that most of the churches of the Association came into existence by this means. The first notice of missionary activity among the western tribes of Indians occurs in 1772, when it was recommended that David Jones be granted an extra allowance because of the expense of employing an interpreter. From his application for a certificate to indicate to the Indians "his good standing with us," it would appear that there had been previous visits to these tribes. The foreign mission interest was fostered almost as soon as there was time for news to arrive of William Carey's establishment of a missionary outpost in the Far East; in 1794 William Rogers was appointed by the Association to collect funds for "the propagation of the gospel among the Hindus."

V

It is clear that the Association could and did act for the churches in matters of common concern external to their own life, and it is equally clear from the Minutes that the Association did not hesitate to intervene in the internal affairs of the churches when such action became necessary.* A primary purpose of the Association, at its

---

*A typical instance of such intervention is recorded in the Minutes of 1731: "The associated brethren, seeing no messengers from Piscataqua as usual and hearing by some of our brethren of the sad and distracted condition of that congregation, they thought it proper to write to them and to appoint Mr. Jenkin Jones and Mr. Joseph Eaton to give them a visit before the winter, which by the blessing of God proved a means to reduce that church to peace and order."

organization in 1707, had been to provide a means whereby the churches could "consult together about such things as were wanting in the churches" and take the necessary steps to "set them in order." And from the beginning, so the records inform us, it was expected that the churches should "fully acquiesce" in the determinations of the Association. This is a point which interpreters of Baptist history in recent generations have found difficult to understand; and their mystification is not surprising, for technical terms with precise meanings are involved.

In all the documents it is affirmed that "each particular church hath a complete power of authority from Jesus Christ . . . to exercise every part of gospel discipline and church government, independent of any other church or assembly whatever," and it is also insisted that an Association is an advisory council and not a "superior judicature" which has a "superior power over the churches concerned."[7] These statements are somewhat deceptive, for they were never meant to suggest that Associations had no powers at all. The Confession of Faith makes it quite clear that Associations were to deal with issues arising from within the life of individual churches, and it also sets the limits to the power of the Association in such matters.

> In cases of difficulties or differences, either in point of doctrine or administration, wherein either the churches in general are concerned or any one church in their peace, union, and edification, or any member or members of any church are injured in or by any proceedings in censures not agreeable to truth and order; it is according to the mind of Christ that many churches holding communion together do by their messengers meet to consider and give their advice in or about the matter of difference . . . ; *howbeit, these messengers assembled are not entrusted with any church-power properly so-called,* or with any jurisdiction over the churches themselves *to exercise any censures* either over any churches or persons, or *to impose their determination* on the churches and officers.

It is the limiting clause that provides the problem of interpretation. What does it mean?

A more complete statement of the basic point of view is contained in the Discipline of 1743.

> Forasmuch as it falls out many times that particular churches have to do with doubtful and difficult matters or differences in point of doctrine or administration . . .; it is according to the mind of Christ that many churches holding communion together should meet by their messengers and delegates to consider of, and to give advice, in or about such matters in difference. . . . And such messengers and

delegates, convened in the name of Christ by the voluntary consent of the several churches in such mutual communion, *may declare and determine* the mind of the Holy Ghost revealed in Scripture concerning things in difference, and *may decree the observation* of things that are true and necessary because revealed and appointed in the Scripture. And the churches will do well to receive, own, and observe such determinations, on the evidence and authority of the mind of the Holy Ghost in them. . . . *Yet such delegates thus assembled are not entrusted or armed with any coercive power* or any superior jurisdiction over the churches concerned, so as *to impose their determinations* on them or their officers *under the penalty of excommunication* or the like.

The key words which have caused confusion are "church-power" and "censures" and "impose."

In the context of the above statements, "church-power" means the "censures" of the church by which a person is excommunicated and his soul delivered to Satan. An Association, having no "church-power," can no more "deliver a soul to Satan" than it can ordain a minister. These are powers which belong to the local church alone. Thus, without the weapon of excommunication and denied the right to compel obedience by calling upon the civil authorities to whip recalcitrants into line, the Association actually has no "coercive power" by which it can "impose" its determinations.* The fundamental consideration, however, which dictated opposition to the notion of an Association's "imposing" its determinations was the insistence that the conscience cannot be coerced. Christ alone is the Lord of the conscience, and therefore a church must not submit willy-nilly to any authority which an Association might be thought to possess, for an Association has no such authority. But, having been persuaded that the conclusions reached by an Association represent the mind of Christ, these conclusions or determinations are to be "owned" and "received" and "acquiesced in" and "observed" by a church.

At this point, the coin is reversed. While an Association may only "determine" and "declare" and not "impose," a church is not free to reject the "advice" and "counsel" of an Association and still remain a member in communion with the other churches of the

---

* "Determination" is another technical term. Neither a church nor an Association legislates in matters of faith and practice. Christ is the legislator. The role of a church and an Association is to judge or interpret or "determine" the mind of Christ as it is made known to them in the Scriptures by the inward illumination of the Holy Spirit. Thus, when a matter is "determined" and "declared" by an Association, the ultimate ground is the authority of Christ and not the authority of the Association.

Association. This is the meaning of the statement that an Association "may decree the observation of things that are true and necessary" and of the parallel insistence that "the churches will do well to receive, own, and observe such determinations." The Association had been formed by "several congregations of our judgment." It was not a collection of miscellaneous churches of varying belief and practice, and no church was subsequently admitted until it first had been ascertained that its "faith and practice" was in harmony with the standards of the Association. The corollary to this, it was frankly recognized, was the right to withdraw fellowship from a church that departs from the accepted faith and practice of the member churches.

The practical implications of this understanding of the role of an Association can be found everywhere in the Minutes of the Philadelphia Association. A good many of the issues that came before the Association had to do with ordination and church "censures." While the Association could neither ordain nor excommunicate, it could "determine"—according to the "gospel rule and order"—the proper *procedure* to be followed in both ordination and excommunication. If a church should then disregard the advice of the Association and persist in its willful course, it could be judged disorderly and fellowship withdrawn.

From a theological point of view, the best statement of the Associational theory is to be found in the "Essay on the Power and Duty of an Association of Churches," which was drafted by Benjamin Griffith in 1749 and "unanimously approved" by the Association after "mature deliberation," and ordered "to be inserted in the Association Book" for the specific purpose of making clear "what power an Association of churches hath and what duty is incumbent on an Association, and [thus] prevent the contempt with which some are ready to treat such an assembly and also to prevent any future generation from claiming more power than they ought—lording it over the churches."* This was the

---

*A common analogy was to compare an Association to a church. While the representatives of the churches meeting together have no "church-power" over the churches or their members, they do themselves constitute, in effect, "one church," having "lawful right" to "act in the name of Christ" and to order their own corporate life. Thus the Essay of 1749 is able to maintain that "in the capacity of a congregational church dealing with her own members, an Association of the delegates of associated churches may exclude and withdraw from defective and unsound or disorderly churches." The Discipline of 1798 states that, since "the union of churches in an Association is a voluntary act . . . like the voluntary confederation of members into a church, it follows that every church stands in the same relation to its Association as a member does to his church."

delicate balance they sought to maintain—seeking to avoid the dangers of both authoritarianism and unfaithfulness, of both ecclesiastical tyranny and ecclesiastical irresponsibility. The essential point is stated in the Discipline compiled by Samuel Jones and adopted by the Association in 1798. After noting that "the associated body may exclude from their connection any church that may act an unworthy part," the Discipline adds:

> Let it not be thought that this power of the Association over the churches in connection with it disannuls or destroys the independence of those churches, for if any church of the associated body should become unsound in their principles, or act irregularly and disorderly, and will not do what may be just and right; such a church will still remain an independent church, though an heterodox and irregular one; but it would be inconsistent and wrong in the Association to suffer such a church to continue among them, since, besides other considerations, they would hereby become partakers of their evil deeds. The Association can take nothing from them but what it gave them. This, in such circumstances, it certainly may and ought to do.

VI

The Association was not a peripheral body. It not only cared for and implemented the common outward concerns of the churches; but it also was an expression of their inward communion in Christ, and it assumed responsibility for preserving their unity in faith and practice, curbing "the wanton abuse of church-power" and affording "assistance and advice in all difficult cases." For such important and weighty matters, the churches were to select as their representatives only the "most capable" among their members, defraying their expenses and looking after their "businesses at home" so that they might be free to attend.[8] The sensitivity of the Association with regard to the importance of having the churches fully represented, if the Association were to have any valid claim to be seeking the mind of Christ for all the churches, is well illustrated in the Minutes of the Association during the American Revolution. With Philadelphia and New York occupied by the British and the common life elsewhere disrupted, many churches found it impossible to send delegates to the annual sessions. In this situation, the Association no longer claimed to speak for all the churches. Whereas it had been accustomed to address the churches as "the ministers and messengers of the several Baptist congregations in Pennsylvania, the Jerseys, and provinces adjacent," it was now careful to specify the churches that were represented, and thus to speak only as "the elders and messengers of the several Baptist churches meeting at Pennepek, Middletown, Piscataqua," etc. It was the sensitivity at this point which ultimately, with the multiplication of churches, led to the multiplication of Associations. If an Association were to act in behalf of the churches, the churches must be represented in the Association.

This problem of proper representation had been developing prior to the Revolution. From the beginning the Philadelphia Association had been an intercolonial body. By 1760 it embraced churches located in the present states of Connecticut, New York, New Jersey, Pennsylvania, Delaware, Virginia, and West Virginia. Maintaining this "national" character became increasingly difficult as the churches continued to multiply and became more widely dispersed. The solution adopted by 1767 was the formation of two subsidiary Associations, the Warren in New England and the Ketochton in Virginia.[9] The disruption of war and the continuing multiplication of churches, however, made it impossible for the Philadelphia Association to continue to serve as the bond of unity among Baptists. Immediately before the Revolution it has been estimated that there were 494 Baptist congregations; twenty years later, in 1795, Isaac Backus estimated the number at 1,152. Left to their own devices, these churches proceeded to organize independent Associations of their own, with the result that by 1800 there were at least 48 local Associations, and thought had to be given to the best means of effecting an alternative national organization.

Ultimately state conventions and a national convention, composed of delegates from the churches, were devised. In the process the sensitivity with regard to the importance of having all the churches fully represented was lost, and the conventions generally have also exercised the right to legislate as well as to "determine." In other respects, the practice of the conventions corresponds to the practice of the early Associations. They act on behalf of the churches in matters of common concern, and they have never surrendered the right to withdraw fellowship from a church as a disciplinary procedure. A curious situation, however, has developed. The practice is no longer supported by a theory. The concept of "the independence of particular churches" has been misunderstood and perverted into a doctrine of "local autonomy," leaving Baptists with no theological basis for organized denominational life. The contradiction between theory and practice is demoralizing enough, but an even more serious consequence is involved. By echoing shibboleths which stemmed from a climate of opinion which found fullest expression in Jacksonian democracy and by constantly indoctrinating the members of the churches in terms of an understanding of the church which contradicts their practice, Baptists are engaged in the ironic task of sowing seeds which can lead only to their own disintegration.

NOTES

[1] R. A. Baker, *Relations Between Northern and Southern Baptists*, p. 8.

[2] *Minutes of the Philadelphia Baptist Association*, ed. A. D. Gillette, pp. 27, 31.

[3] *Ibid.*, p. 121. See also p. 25.

[4] *Ibid.*, p. 27. Examples of such certificates, properly notarized, can be found in the Minutes for 1758 and 1762, *ibid.*, pp. 77, 86.

[5] *Ibid.*, pp. 82, 283, 332. See also p. 114.

[6] Garnett Ryland, *The Baptists of Virginia, 1699-1926*, p. 12. See also pp. 9-11.

[7] These quotations are from the "Essay on the Power and Duty of an Association," *Minutes*, pp. 60-61.

[8] *Ibid.*, pp. 25, 28-29.

[9] As early as 1751 the Philadelphia Association had provided leadership in organizing the Charleston Association in the "far country" of the Carolinas. Having little expectation of delegates being able to be present, the connection with Charleston was maintained by "correspondence."

3
The Ministry: Pastoral Call and Ordination

All Christians are called to be ministers. This is the meaning of the priesthood or mutual ministry of all believers. All Christians are called to bear witness to Christ, to testify to the forgiveness they have found, to pray for one another, and to give themselves in loving service to their neighbors. This is the call to the ministry, and it is a call that comes to all Christians.

In addition to this general calling of all Christians, there is a more specific calling of some Christians to the work of the pastoral ministry—the calling of an individual to be the leader of a congregation, charging him with responsibility to lead the congregation in the public worship of God, to instruct it in Christian truth, to watch over its members in Christian love with words of encouragement and admonition, and to guide the congregation in all its corporate activities.

The necessity for this more specific calling arises in part from a recognition that, if the congregation is to be properly instructed, led, guided, and admonished, one of the number must be so freed from other responsibilities that he will have time to devote himself to the study of Scripture and to become skilled in ascertaining God's will for his people. The necessity for this specific calling also stems in part from an awareness that, if confusion is to be avoided and order established, one member must be chosen to assume certain responsibilities on behalf of all the members. If everyone attempted to lead the congregation in worship, for example, chaos would prevail. This was a point emphasized by John Calvin in the *Ecclesiastical Ordinances* of 1541: "In order that nothing happen confusedly in the church, no one is to enter upon this [pastoral] office without a calling."[1] Lastly, this insistence arose as an expression of the principle that what belongs to all shall be exercised by no one without the consent of all. The ministry belongs to the whole church, and no one may perform any ministerial act in a representative or corporate capacity unless he has been properly called thereto by the church.

I

The call to the pastoral ministry is a call of the church. As Morgan Edwards, the earliest Baptist historian, put it: "The election or outward call of a person to the ministry is an act of his church."[2] The pastor, to be sure, is not the servant of the congregation by virtue of this calling, for he receives his marching orders, as do all his fellow "priests," from the Lord. The relationship may be stated in this way. The call is "by the church" but it is "from Christ." Thus, the pastor does not become the servant of the church as a result of his election any more than "a captain (by leave of the general) chosen by the band of soldiers is the servant of his band."[3] With this reservation in mind, it is clear, nonetheless, that the essence of the pastor's calling is derived basically and fundamentally from the act of the congregation.

There is, of course, an inward as well as an outward call. John Calvin, when insisting that no one "may be accounted a true minister of the church" unless "he be regularly called to it," acknowledged that he was speaking of the "external call which belongs to the public order of the church" and that he was "passing over that secret call, of which every minister is conscious to himself before God, but which is not known to the church." The "secret call," he continued, "is the honest testimony of our heart that we accept the office offered to us, not from ambition or avarice, or any other unlawful motive, but from a sincere fear of God and an ardent zeal for the edification of the church." But, since this secret call can be known with certainty only to God, it is necessary to regard even one "who enters upon his office with an evil conscience . . . [as] duly called, provided his iniquity is not discovered."[4]

The early Congregationalists and Baptists shared this general Reformation point of view. "No man," the *Cambridge Platform* declared, "may take the honor of a church officer unto himself, but he that was called of God, as was Aaron." The calling of the apostles and prophets was an *"immediate"* calling by God, but "this manner of calling ended with them." Since apostolic times, one's calling to an office in the church is *"mediate,* by the church."[5] This point of view is equally apparent in early Baptist records. Baptists, for example, were reminded "to make inquiry among themselves" to discover if they had "any young persons hopeful for the ministry and inclinable for learning;" and if so, to make provision for their education with the expectation that ultimately they might make public trial of their gifts prior to being called and ordained. Furthermore, a church that was "destitute" of a minister and with no available "supply" from a neighboring church was urged to "pitch" upon some person in the congregation who gave promise of being useful in the ministry and to give him "a solemn invitation to the work of the ministry on trial." He was first to be put on "private trial," and then permitted to preach in public. "After which, if it should appear that his rod, like Aaron's, buds, blossoms, and bears fruit, he is to be set apart by ordination that he may perform every part of the sacred function."[6]

The Congregationalists and Baptists also insisted that this outward call must be accompanied by an inward call which was defined, in a manner which closely paralleled Calvin's definition, as "a zeal for the glory of God in the salvation of the souls of men, and a strong desire to be made useful in that way, with a persuasion of God's designation of the person for the office."[7] The inward call was made manifest in certain outward "gifts" and "virtues" which were to be "tried" and "proved." While there was a slightly greater confidence that the inward call could be tested, the "trying" did not differ in any significant fashion from the examination which Calvin instituted at Geneva.[8]

Among Baptists, after an individual had been "licensed to preach" and his "gifts" had been "tried" and "proved," it was proper for the church to proceed to ordain him so that he might perform all the acts and functions of the pastoral office. In a general sense, to ordain is to appoint, to decree, to order, to command, to establish. In church life, to ordain is to appoint and to install formally an individual in a specific office, and to authorize him thereby to assume certain responsibilities on behalf of the other members of the church. Ordination to the pastoral ministry is the appointment and installation of an individual as the leader of a specific congregation and thus represents the completion and formalization of the call of the church.[9] It does not confer a special status before God or impart a unique and indelible character to the person ordained. The essential feature of the pastoral ministry is a pastoral relationship to a church. It is this relationship that ordination confirms and formalizes.

Initially among Baptists a person was ordained to the pastoral ministry of a specific local church. Morgan Edwards put this fact bluntly when he said: "Every minister is such by an act of his own church. No man or set of men can do that for a church. Nor yet one church for another." [10] When the person so ordained ceased to be pastor of that particular church, his ordination had no further validity. If another church wished to call him as its pastor, it was necessary for him to be ordained once again to the new office. Thus, ordination was restricted both in scope and in time—a restriction which also found expression in the ordaining of deacons for a definite term of office.

There were two factors which ultimately led to a modification of the early practice of ordaining an individual only to the pastoral ministry of a specific church. The first was the quite understandable desire of churches to be able to call a pastor with the assurance that he was regarded by other Baptist churches as fully qualified for the pastoral ministry. Consequently, men began to be ordained to the pastoral ministry at large among Baptist churches. It remained true that the validity of ordination depended upon a pastoral relationship to a church. Thus, when a person ceased to have such a relationship, his ordination was at best in abeyance. Nevertheless, having been ordained to a general pastoral ministry and certified as fully qualified for the work of a pastor, he did not need to be reordained when called to another church. The procedure, then, was for his ordination to be confirmed and his pastoral relationship to the new church established by a service of installation. The second factor that led to this newer practice was the equally understandable desire of many churches to ordain one who had been raised in their midst, even though the reason for his ordination was the call he had received to be pastor of some other church. And it is quite fitting and proper that his home church should have this opportunity to set him apart for the work of the pastoral ministry.

II

Individuals have found their way into the pastoral ministry through various paths. Frequently the first step is taken as a result of some word spoken by a pastor, a deacon, a church school teacher, or some other member of the church. Only occasionally has the initial step been the consequence of an immediate and direct summons from the whole church, calling upon a person to enter the ministry.

An urgent summons of the latter type, running counter to the individual's own inclination, finds classic illustration in John

Knox's induction into the ministry. Knox had been serving as tutor to some "gentlemen's children," and in that capacity he had taken refuge in the besieged castle at St. Andrews. As part of his program of instruction he taught the Scriptures to his young charges, lecturing to them with such power that John Rough, the castle preacher, besought him to preach in his stead. Knox refused, saying that he had no vocation and that he was unwilling to "run where God had not called him."

Whereupon John Rough, with the consent of the whole company, preached a sermon on the power that "the congregation (how small that ever it was, passing the number of two or three) had above any man in whom they supposed and espied the gifts of God to be, and how dangerous it was to refuse and not hear the voice of such as desired to be instructed."

And then, speaking directly to Knox, he said, "Brother, ye shall not be offended, albeit that I speak unto you that which I have in charge, even from all those that are here present, which is this: In the name of God and of his son Jesus Christ, and in the name of these that presently calls you by my mouth, I charge you, that ye refuse not this holy vocation, but that as ye have regard to the glory of God, the increase of Christ his kingdom, the edification of your brethren, and the comfort of me, whom ye understand well enough to be oppressed by the multitude of labors, that ye take upon you the public office and charge of preaching, even as ye look to avoid God's heavy displeasure and desire that he shall multiply his graces with you."

Then, turning to those present, Rough said, "Was not this your charge to me? And do ye not approve this vocation?" They answered, "It was, and we approve it." At this, Knox burst into tears and withdrew. From that day until the day that "he was compelled to present himself to the public place of preaching," his conduct, it was reported, testified to "the grief and trouble of his heart." [11]

In more recent times, George W. Truett provides an equally dramatic instance of a person brought into the ministry against his will. As a young man in Whitewright, Texas, Truett was repeatedly urged to become a minister, but he was adamant in his determination to be a lawyer. On a Saturday in 1890 he was struck by the large attendance at the covenant meeting, thinking it singular for there to be a house full of people on a Saturday. He soon discovered the reason for this, reporting the sequence of events in his own words.

> When they got through with all the rest of the church conference . . . ,
> the oldest deacon . . . rose up and began to talk. . . . "There is such a
> thing as a church duty when the whole church must act. There is such
> a thing as an individual duty when the individual must face duty for
> himself. But it is my deep conviction as it is yours—for we have talked
> much one with another—that this church has a duty to perform and
> that we have waited late and long to get about it. I move, therefore,
> that this church call a presbytery to ordain Brother George W. Truett
> to the full work of the gospel ministry.

Truett protested. He implored them to desist. He asked them to
wait six months. But the church refused to heed his pleas. The
motion was carried, the presbytery was summoned, and George W.
Truett was ordained.[12]

Not everyone, of course, has been dragooned into the ministry.
Many have responded willingly to the call of the church. John
Bunyan, for example, was an itinerant tinker who wandered about
the countryside plying his trade and witnessing to his faith. In
1655, about two years after he had joined the church at Bedford, "he
was asked by the brethren to speak a word of exhortation in their
gatherings," and responding to their request he "did discover
[reveal] his gift among them." He was licensed to preach and
"began to go out with the brethren who went into the country to
teach." More and more it became apparent to himself and others
that his true vocation was the pastoral ministry. It was not until the
end of his twelve years imprisonment, however, that the church
issued a call to him and he was finally ordained.[13]

Bunyan provides a transition to what was probably a more
common path into the ministry, for Bunyan's conversion had
expressed itself in an irresistible impulse to share in the work of
redemption by making known the victory that had been won
within his own heart. Charles G. Finney provides a familiar
illustration of the conversion experience itself giving the impetus
which thrust one into the ministry. A moderately successful lawyer
in upstate New York who was something of a skeptic, Finney
underwent a soul-shattering religious experience which brought
his legal career to an end. The morning after the resolution of his
inner spiritual crisis, a man appeared in his office and said, "Mr.
Finney, do you recollect that my cause is to be tried at ten o'clock
this morning?" To which Finney replied, "Deacon B——, I have a
retainer from the Lord Jesus Christ to plead his cause, and I cannot
plead yours."[14]

James Martineau found his way into the ministry through a
similar conversion experience. Horace Bushnell's conversion was

less dramatic than Martineau's, but he was able to date when it occurred in "a little bedroom" of his college dormitory, and it caused him to give up the law for the Gospel. Phillips Brooks's conversion, on the other hand, was a gradual awakening, accompanied by a slowly maturing purpose which led him into the ministry. It was much the same story with William Carey, who "could never date the day and hour of his new birth." [15]

Although nothing could be more natural than a conversion experience expressing itself in terms of the pastoral vocation, external influence often contributed to this outcome. Sometimes it arose from a desire to emulate the one who had been instrumental in bringing him to a new birth. This undoubtedly was true of Robert Robinson, who called George Whitfield his "spiritual father." [16] It was true of John Eliot, whose "spiritual life was kindled" in the household of Thomas Hooker. "When I came to this blessed family," he said, "I then saw, and never before, the power of godliness in its lively vigor and efficacy." [17] It was true of many of Finney's converts. During 1830 nearly every boy in the Rochester Free Academy was converted as a result of Finney's labors, and more than forty of them ultimately became ministers. [18] But the key influence in many instances was exerted by parents. It probably was not without significance that the mother of Phillips Brooks desired above all else that he should become a minister. The sons of Heman Humphrey Barbour, probate judge of Hartford, Connecticut, provide a conspicuous illustration of the influence of a father, for of his six sons by two wives, five entered the ministry. [19]

Although the desire of parents and the influence of the home environment can frequently be seen as a decisive factor in an ultimate decision to enter the ministry, the parent's expectations were not always fulfilled without a struggle. Lyman Beecher, who had been led into the ministry through the instrumentality of Timothy Dwight at Yale, expected that all his sons would become preachers. They tended to follow the line of least resistance and enter theological seminary, but —perhaps as a result of their father being tried for heresy—they all were alienated by the doctrines of orthodoxy and were tempted to turn from a ministerial career. Charles Beecher actually became a shipping clerk for a time, and Thomas K. Beecher spent some years teaching school before he could be persuaded to be ordained. For Henry Ward Beecher, the resolution came while he was in seminary. He had been assailed by doubts and was uncertain as to any message that he might have. But one "blessed morning," he tells us,

> it pleased God to reveal to my wandering soul the idea that it was his
> nature to love man in his sins for the sake of helping him out of them;
> that he did not do it out of compliment to Christ, or to a law, or a plan
> of salvation, but from the fullness of a great heart; . . . that he was not
> furious with wrath toward the sinner, but pitied him—in short, that
> he felt toward me as my mother felt toward me to whose eyes my
> wrongdoing brought tears, who never pressed me so close to her as
> when I had done wrong.

In describing this illumination which had come to him so quietly
and yet so suddenly, Henry Ward Beecher comments: "I was like
the man in the story to whom the fairy gave a purse with a single
piece of money in it, which he found always came again as soon as
he had spent it. I thought I knew at least one thing to preach. I
found it included everything."[20]

More often than not, it is the interplay of various influences
that leads an individual into the ministry. This was the experience
of Adoniram Judson. His father was a minister, and we may
assume the importance of the home environment. But while he was
at Brown University, there was no indication that he was
considering a ministerial vocation. After graduation he joined a
theatrical troupe in New York City. One night in a country inn, the
man in the next room died. The next morning Judson discovered
that it was a friend, a deistical member of the class ahead of him at
Brown, who had died during the night. Deeply troubled, Judson
left the troupe and returned home. Shortly thereafter, two
professors from the theological seminary at Andover who were
visiting his father urged him to enter the seminary. At first he
refused and took a teaching job instead. A month later he changed
his mind, entering the seminary "not as a professor of religion and
candidate for the ministry, but as a person deeply in earnest on the
subject and desirous of arriving at the truth." The sequel is told by
a friend:

> I have often heard Dr. Judson speak of his introduction to Andover
> and of the state of utter darkness and almost despair in which he was
> at the time. I have also heard him tell of the gradual change which
> came over him. . . .
> There was none of his characteristic impetuosity exhibited in his
> conversion; and he had none of those overpowering, Bunyan-like
> exercises, either before or after, that would be looked for in a person of
> his ardent temperament. He was prayerful, reflective, and studious of
> proofs; and gradually faith, trust in God, and finally a hope through
> the merits of Christ, took possession of his soul; he scarcely knew
> how. And from the moment that he fully believed, I think he never
> doubted. He said he felt as sure that he was an entirely new creature,

actuated by new motives and governed by new principles, as he was sure of his own existence. . . . The change, though gradual, was too marked, too entire, to admit of a moment's doubt. He had no exercises on the subject of entering the ministry; it became a matter of course immediately on his indulging a hope.

In Judson various influences quite obviously were at work—home and family, the death of a friend, the visit of the two theological professors, his seminary studies.[21]

While there is no single path that has led individuals to offer themselves for the work of the pastoral ministry in the conviction that it is God's will that they should make themselves useful in this way, in the end the actual "call" must come from the church. It cannot be otherwise, for a pastor is the pastor of a church. His is not the general ministry of all believers. It is a specialized ministry in which he acts as the representative of all the members of the congregation. The essential feature of his calling is this relationship to a church.

III

It should be acknowledged, however, that neither Protestants in general nor Baptists in particular have always been clear with regard to the nature of the pastoral ministry. Any precise understanding always tends to become ambiguous and even obscured and forgotten with the passage of time, and this has been true of the understanding which governed the meaning assigned to the role of the pastor. This misunderstanding was furthered by the actual sequence of events which usually led to a person's decision to enter the pastoral ministry. While the initiative theoretically (and in the end, actually) belonged to the church, in practice the initiative most frequently was taken by the individual who presented himself to the church as a candidate for the ministry. Ultimately the individual's initiative was given a measure of structural theological support in a large segment of Protestantism by a developing insistence that a direct and immediate inner call should be the first step in the path which brought one into the ministry. Instead of the outward call being confirmed by an inward response to that call, the progression was reversed so that the outward call became a recognition and confirmation of the inward call. There were other factors, of course, which fostered this development.

In times of religious excitement, unrest, and turmoil, there always have been persons who have felt their call to preach to be by the Holy Spirit, quite apart from any church. The Reformation era constituted one such period, and a typical instance of a sudden call to preach during the Reformation era is reported by E. B. Bax in *The Rise and Fall of the Anabaptists.*

> A peasant, Hans Ber of Alten-Erlangen, rose from his bed one night and began to put on his clothes. "Whither goest thou?" asked his wife. "I know not, God knoweth," was his answer. She entreated him to stay with the words: "What evil have I done thee? Stay here and help me nourish my little children." "Dear wife," he replied, "harry me not with the things of time. God bless thee. I will from hence, that I may learn the will of the Lord."[22]

George Fox, the founder of the Quakers, was only one among many who felt the call to preach by a special motion of the Holy Spirit during the religious chaos which was so conspicuous a feature of the tumultuous years of the English Civil Wars and Commonwealth. So widespread was the phenomenon of unlettered rustics and mechanics—to say nothing of women—forsaking their work to become itinerant preachers, that the more sober religious elements of the population became greatly alarmed. One versifier expressed a common conviction in this couplet:

> When tinkers preach and women pray,
> The fiends in hell make holiday.

This was not a pastoral ministry in which these men and women were engaged. It was not carried on in relationship to any church. But in the minds of many it did establish a norm in terms of an immediate call to preach for any ministry. It was highly individualistic, for no man or group of men was considered to have the right to sit in judgment upon the "call" and to say nay to the Lord. For good or ill, this heritage was to live on in the English-speaking world, and in modified form it was to penetrate many of the conventional churches during the eighteenth century under the influence of the Evangelical Revival.

The influence of the Evangelical Revival, known as the Great Awakening in the English colonies of North America, can best be seen in terms of Gilbert Tennent's sermon on "The Danger of an Unconverted Ministry."[23] The sermon was a denunciation of "Pharisee-Teachers" who are "letter-learned" but unconverted, having had "no experience of a special work of the Holy Ghost upon their own souls." They are like "dead dogs that can't bark," being neither inclined to nor fitted for the essential work of the ministry.

> Is a blind man fit to be a guide in a very dangerous way? Is a dead man

fit to bring others to life? A mad man fit to give counsel in a matter of life and death? . . . Is an ignorant rustic, that has never been at sea in his life, fit to be a pilot, to keep vessels from being dashed to pieces upon rocks and sand-banks? Isn't an unconverted minister like a man who would learn others to swim before he has learn'd it himself, and so is drowned in the act and dies like a fool?

With his condemnation of "the ministry of natural man" who have only "the name of a minister, with a band and a black coat or gown" to commend them, Tennent was insisting that they should have no more than that experience of grace which should be common to all Christians. But, given a situation in which many church members had had no unusual experience of grace, it was not difficult to draw the conclusion that some special work of God was necessary for the ministry.

Tennent spoke with scorn of "hireling" ministers who made a trade of the ministry, and it was but a short step from this characterization to an insistence that true ministers should have some immediate inner call which would distinguish them from the hirelings. Whether or not Tennent took this step himself is not clear, but it was taken by others. Throughout much of American Protestantism there came to be an increasing insistence that the fundamental ground of pastoral ministry was an inward call of the individual that had its own validity quite apart from the outward call of the church.

While one can appreciate the earnest concerns which led to this shift in definition of the pastoral ministry, the consequences of the shift were disastrous. It tended to undermine any notion of an ordered church life. It obscured the fact that the ministry belongs to the church, and that every Christian is called as a responsible "priest" to share that ministry. It obliterated the representative character of the pastoral office and fostered a growing cleavage between pastor and people by cultivating the essentially Catholic notion that ordination either recognizes or confers a unique and indelible character that existed quite independently of any pastoral relationship. Finally, it denied the fundamental conviction of Baptists that the most appropriate instrument for ascertaining the will of God is the corporate inquiry of the whole congregation. If this developing clericalism is to be arrested, it would seem to be imperative for Baptists to make clear once again their basic convictions concerning the church and its ministry, as they are expressed in their understanding of what is implied in ordination as an act of the church and an establishment of a relationship between pastor and people, in which ministry is conducted.

Increase Mather pointed to the very essence of ordination some 250 years ago when he declared: "To say that a *Wandering Levite* who has no flock is a pastor is as good sense as to say that he who has no children is a father."[24]

NOTES

[1] J. K. S. Reid, ed., *Calvin: Theological Treatises*, vol. xxii (Library of Christian Classics, Philadelphia, 1954), p. 58.

[2] Morgan Edwards, *The Customs of Primitive Churches* (Philadelphia, 1774), p. 17.

[3] Perry Miller, *Orthodoxy in Massachusetts* (Cambridge, Mass., 1933), p. 178.

[4] H. R. Niebuhr and D. D. Williams, eds., *The Ministry in Historical Perspectives* (New York, 1956), p. 141.

[5] Williston Walker, ed., *The Creeds and Platforms of Congregationalism* (New York, 1893), p. 214.

[6] A. D. Gillette, ed., *Minutes of the Philadelphia Baptist Association, 1707-1807* (Philadelphia, 1851), p. 27. *A Short Treatise of Church Discipline*, appended to *A Confession of Faith* (Philadelphia, 1743), p. 11. *Baptist Confession of Faith and a Summary of Church Discipline* (Charlestown, S. C., 1831), p. 133.

[7] *Ibid.*, p. 195.

[8] *Calvin: Theological Treatises*, p. 59.

[9] Ordination as the formalizing of the pastoral relationship in terms of call and response was sometimes obscured in the practice of some churches. It usually was required that a person be examined and recommended for ordination by a council of ministers or by a superintendent or bishop, and this was commonly regarded as the initial step in the process which leads to ordination. But even so, the theoretically indispensable prerequisite to ordination and the essential feature of a minister's calling was the action of a local congregation in electing or accepting him as its minister. This election or acceptance was generally regarded as more important than the act of ordination itself. *The Ministry in Historical Perspectives*, p. 139.

[10] Morgan Edwards, *op. cit.*, p. 17.

[11] W. C. Dickinson, ed., *John Knox's History of the Reformation in Scotland*, (New York, 1950), vol. i. pp. 52f.

[12] P. W. James, *George W. Truett: A Biography* (New York, 1939), p. 48.

[13] John Brown, *John Bunyan* (Boston, 1888), pp. 110f.

[14] Cited in W. S. Hudson, *The Great Tradition of the American Churches* (New York, 1953), p. 90.

[15] J. E. Carpenter, *James Martineau* (Boston, 1906), pp. 23-25. Horace Bushnell, *Life and Letters* (New York, 1880), p. 59. A. V. G. Allen, *Life and Letters of Phillips Brooks* (New York, 1900), vol. i, p. 140. S. P. Carey, *William Carey* (London, 1923), p. 30.

[16] George Dyer, *Memoirs of the Life and Writings of Robert Robinson* (London, 1796), p. 18.

[17] Convers Francis, *Life of John Eliot* (New York, 1860), p. 6.

[18] V. R. Edman, *Finney Lives On* (New York, 1951), p. 76.

[19] "Clarence A. Barbour," article in *Dictionary of American Biography*, vol. xxii, Supplement Two (New York, 1958).

[20] "Charles Beecher," "Edward Beecher," "Henry Ward Beecher" and "Thomas K. Beecher," articles in *Dictionary of American Biography*, vol. ii (New York, 1929).

[21] Francis Wayland, *Memoir of the Life and Labors of the Rev. Adoniram Judson, D.D.* (Boston, 1853), vol. i, pp. 26, 36-37.

[22] E. B. Bax, *The Rise and Fall of the Anabaptists* (London, 1903), pp. 33f.

[23] M. W. Armstrong *et al*, eds., *The Presbyterian Enterprise* (Philadelphia, 1956), pp. 40-44.

[24] Quoted by C. C. Goen, *Revivalism and Separatism in New England, 1740–1800* (New Haven, 1962), p. 9.

PART II
ISSUES
HISTORICALLY
CONSIDERED

4
Baptists, the Pilgrim Fathers, and the American Revolution

Between 1770 and 1800 Baptists emerged from relative obscurity to become the largest denomination in America.

This thirty-year period is known as the age of the American Revolution. It began in 1770 with the "Boston Massacre" and other skirmishes preceding the Declaration of Independence. It included the seven-year war that followed, the makeshift political arrangements of the Articles of Confederation, the struggle to draft and then to secure the adoption of the federal Constitution, and finally the time of testing in the last decade of the century when it was not yet clear whether or not the new nation could gain sufficient stability to survive.

These thirty years from 1770 to 1800 were a troubled time for most American churches. The Presbyterian General Assembly in 1798 echoed a common lament when it bewailed the "general dereliction of religious principle and practice among our fellow citizens" and complained of a "visible and prevailing impiety and contempt for the laws and institutions of religion." Similar views were voiced by leading Congregational and Episcopal divines. Lyman Beecher reported that "irreligion hath become in all parts of our land, alarmingly prevalent," with "the name of God . . . blasphemed, the bible . . . denounced, the sabbath . . . profaned, the public worship of God . . . neglected." So depressed had Bishop Samuel Provoost of the Episcopal Church become that in 1801 he relinquished his episcopal duties, being convinced that the church would "die out with the old colonial families."[1] Baptists, on the other hand, had little cause to express such gloomy forebodings about their prospects.

Baptist experience during the politically troubled years from 1770 to 1800 was in marked contrast to that of denominations which in 1770 had enjoyed preeminence in numbers, prestige, and influence. Unlike the denominations which were lamenting a prevailing impiety and neglect of public worship, Baptists had been and were experiencing a sweeping surge of growth. Instead of diminishing in numbers, Baptists had increased. They had increased at such an astonishing rate that by 1800 Baptists had outpaced all other religious bodies to become the largest religious group in America, with twice as many adherents as the next largest denomination.[2]

Such a startling and even disconcerting countertrend among Baptists requires some explanation. How does one account for this remarkable Baptist growth when other denominations were suffering demoralization and decline?

I

To measure the magnitude of the Baptist achievement from 1770 to 1800, it is necessary to go back to the preceding thirty years to place the period in proper perspective.

As late as 1740 Baptists in America were a small, undistinguished, and little-noted religious group. There were only a handful of churches in New England (three in Connecticut and eight in Massachusetts), a similar handful in the middle colonies (five in New Jersey and six in Pennsylvania), and a still smaller handful in the southern colonies. Even Rhode Island, which traditionally had been regarded as a center of Baptist strength, had only one "regular" Baptist church, the others being Seventh Day or Six Principle churches outside of what was to be the mainstream of Baptist life.

Thirty years later, in 1770 the number of Baptist churches was still modest. Their rate of increase, to be sure, from a very small base, was impressive. While not yet regarded as a serious rival by the major denominations, Baptists nonetheless were exhibiting unusual vigor and vitality. This was true in New England where the new vitality first manifested itself. It also was true in the South where, after 1755, the contagious enthusiasm of Baptist preachers from New England began to awaken a growing response.

In retrospect it is clear that by 1770 Baptists had several things going for them—increasing numbers, new leaders, a new spirit, and a new sense of mission, purpose, and destiny. In one way or another all these were related to the "Separate" Congregationalists of New England. Even in the South the multiplying number of Baptists was the result of the vitality introduced by New England "Separates" turned Baptist. In 1755, Sandy Creek, North Carolina, became the base from which the revivals associated with Shubal Stearns radiated throughout the North Carolina piedmont and the adjacent counties of southside Virginia. Stearns's brother-in-law, Daniel Marshall, also from New England, extended the sphere of vigorous Baptist evangelistic activity into South Carolina and Georgia. Later, John Leland, of Connecticut, was to bring a new burst of Baptist zeal to the central piedmont area of Virginia. These successes in the South and those of lesser degree in the middle colonies pointed back to New England where the shape of things to come had been fashioned.

The story of the pre-1770 shift in Baptist fortunes begins with the Great Awakening in New England and with the attempts that were made to contain the fervor generated by the Awakening. The containment efforts led to tension, conflict, division, and in the end to a steady drift of Congregationalists into the Baptist fold.

The enthusiasm spawned by the Awakening created tension primarily at two points.[3] The first was the insistence of partisans of the Awakening that church membership should be restricted to those who could testify to their own personal experience of the miracle of grace. The second was the desire of the "awakened" to have "awakening" preachers as their pastors. The pattern of conflict varied from parish to parish. Where an "awakening" preacher was firmly entrenched as pastor, there was less likelihood of overt conflict. But when a new pastor was to be called, ordained, and installed, ample opportunities existed in the political-ecclesiastical arrangements of the New England system to thwart the desires of the "awakened." This was true even when the partisans of the Awakening were able to marshal the support of the church membership. When any of these opportunities for obstruction were utilized, the eager enthusiasts of the revival were quick to assert that the spiritual energy released by the Awakening should not be subject to restraint by an unregenerate parish majority composed of nonchurch members, nor by an extra-congregational ecclesiastical authority (most commonly by ministerial associations), nor by acts of the General Court. As sturdy individualists, members of the "awakened" faction were especially scornful of the notion that God operated through an elite composed of "the learned clergy and the upper social orders." In the Awakening, so they believed, God had "demonstrated his willingness, in this New World, to by-pass these groups" and to make his will known directly to "His chosen saints of whatever order of society or learning."[4]

When "awakened" Congregationalists failed to reform their parish church and especially when they were denied the right to ordain the pastor of their choice, many proceeded to withdraw and form a "Separate" congregation of their own. Subject to constant legal and ecclesiastical harassment by representatives of the Standing Order, these "Separate" Congregationalists tended to gravitate into the ranks of the Baptists.[5] This drift to the Baptists was equally true of disenchanted Congregationalists who did not have an opportunity to take the intermediate step of forming or joining a "Separate" church.

It is not surprising that there should have been this drift to the Baptists, for the disaffected Congregationalists found the Baptist churches congenial at almost every point. Baptists were firmly committed to a church membership restricted to convinced believers. Baptist churches were democratically governed and not subject to control by any unregenerate parish majority. Baptists had long defended their right to religious liberty. Theologically, "Separates" and Baptists were of one mind, and the shift to the practice of believer's baptism was neither difficult to make nor difficult to justify on the basis of convictions which had been the occasion for the "Separates'" break with the churches of the Standing Order.

As a consequence of the drift to the Baptists, the once powerful "Separate" movement in New England withered away after 1754.[6] The former "Separate" Congregationalists constituted a new breed of Baptists. They were neither accustomed to nor ready to accept a sectarian status and the social stigma such status entailed. Many had been and were persons of some stature in their respective communities, and they were not prepared to submit easily to infractions of what they considered as their rights.

As important as the new members Baptists garnered in the years prior to 1770 were the new leaders they acquired, leaders who were brash, self-confident, and self-assertive. By 1760 the new leaders had seized the initiative. Hitherto Baptists had sought little more than "mere survival within the Puritan system."[7] The new leadership, however, was not content to maintain a defensive posture and hope that by good behavior they would be able to retain the concessions granted them by the Standing Order. The new leaders had a larger goal than mere survival in mind. Instead of seeking concessions, they were determined to reform the whole New England system. Far from being passive, they were bold and aggressive, even truculent, in their attacks on the Standing Order and in their demand that it be restructured on the basis of full and complete religious liberty.

As was true in the South, the new Baptist leaders in New England were former "Separate" Congregationalists, men who had sharpened their propagandist weapons and developed their leadership skills in the guerrilla wars they had waged both within and against the established Congregational churches. The most conspicuous of the new leaders was Isaac Backus. It was Backus more than anyone else who infused the Baptists of New England with a new sense of mission, purpose, and destiny; a sense of mission, purpose, and destiny which was first identified with the "errand into the wilderness" of the Pilgrim Fathers, and then later was linked to the mission, purpose, and destiny of the emerging nation.

During the decade prior to 1770 Backus was busy fashioning what can only be described as a propagandist coup. Far from being upstarts, he insisted, Baptists were the true heirs of the first settlers. Unlike the representatives of the Standing Order who had defected from the first principles of New England, Baptists had remained constant in their devotion to the founding fathers. In doctrine, in church government, and especially in their defense of religious liberty, Baptists were the faithful children, the loyal descendants, of those who had fled oppression in their native land to establish a haven of liberty in the American wilderness.

In tract after tract, Backus depicted New England as "the land to which our ancestors fled for religious liberty."[8] It is true, he acknowledged, that it was not long before a "warping off" from the principles of the founders began to take place. But, Backus noted, this "warping off" began quite accidentally and unintentionally. New Englanders were scarcely aware at the outset how unscripturally they were confounding church and state together, for they continued to make strenuous efforts in the early years to keep them distinct.[9] As time passed, however, those who had left England to find freedom to worship God according to their own consciences became as fond of a compulsory religious uniformity as those from whom they fled. Fortunately, Backus observed, "nothing teaches like experience." Consequently, it is much "easier now to discover the mistakes" that were made "than it was for them to do it then."[10]

The most interesting and audacious propagandist item Backus produced was his *History of New England,* a detailed account of the mistakes that had been made and of the oppressions that flowed therefrom.[11] His purpose in compiling the history, as he noted in the Preface to the first volume, was to document the fact that "oppression on religious accounts was not of the first principles of New England but was an intruder that came in afterward." This point was reiterated in the second volume, with Backus again noting that "the first planters of New England requested no more than equal liberty of conscience" and that "on this foundation was New England planted. . . ."[12] This was the basic premise Backus had sought to establish in his tracts, but he also wished to pin down a larger contention. Taken as a whole, his *History of New England* was a remarkable tour de force, for Backus had the audacity to add as a subtitle: "with Particular Reference to the Denomination of Christians Called Baptists." The clear inference was that Baptists provided the central thread, the continuing witness, the true succession in the history of New England.

The mind-set cultivated by the propagandist campaign did two very important things for Baptists. By identifying themselves with those who first came to New England, Baptists gained status and respectability. This, in turn, facilitated their evangelistic efforts and made it much easier to win new recruits. It also made their attacks on the Standing Order immeasurably more effective. In the second place, it gave Baptists a larger sense of mission. They came to view themselves as instruments of a new reformation that would restore New England to its first foundation. Through the Baptists the whole political-ecclesiastical order of New England was to be remodeled and reconstituted to bring it into conformity with the original purpose of the "errand into the wilderness."

By their accounts of how the memory of the Fathers had been dishonored by past and present oppressions, Baptists sought to prick the consciences of leading representatives of the Standing Order. In even more demanding tones, Baptists reminded the Massachusetts leadership of the "charter liberties" guaranteed tender consciences by the Charter of 1691. In their demand for religious liberty, Baptists were touching the New England establishment at a vulnerable point. Ever since Massachusetts Bay had lost its original charter, New England Congregationalists had utilized carefully qualified arguments for religious liberty as a means of defending their privileges against Anglican encroachments, and this had led to some modification of their practice. Still the basic system remained unimpaired. So commonplace had the appeal to religious liberty become that in 1765, when John Adams became alarmed by the twin threats of "stamping" and "episcopizing," he felt neither hesitancy nor embarrassment in attempting to rally public opinion with the peremptory summons: "Let the pulpit resound with the doctrines and sentiments of religious liberty," for there is "direct and formal design on foot, to enslave all America."[13] The Baptist response to such rhetoric was to press the Congregationalists ever more firmly to bring their practice into accord with their profession.

The Baptist propaganda campaign was more successful in winning new members than it was in effecting change in the New England church-state system. Still it did succeed in placing the Congregational establishment on the defensive. Ezra Stiles, for example, in 1760 felt it necessary to defend the liberality of the New England way in his *Discourse on the Christian Union*. This was an indirect reply, for Stiles blandly ignored specific complaints that were being made. Instead he simply affirmed that New England's ecclesiastical arrangements were fully consonant with a profession of religious liberty. He described "the happy policy of establishing one sect without infringing on the essential rights of others" which "is peculiar to the three New England provinces where Congregationalism is the establishment." The secret of this "happy" state of affairs is two-fold. First, the congregational polity of the established churches provides its own guarantee of liberty and guard against tyranny. There can be no centralized ecclesiastical despotism, since "each congregation had an unlimited, absolute, and self-determining power in the choice of their own officers." Second, other churches are permitted to exist, and while all inhabitants are taxed for the support of religion, certified members of recognized dissenting groups can assign their taxes to the church of their choice. This latitude, Stiles concluded, makes possible "the friendly cohabitation of all."[14]

Stiles's idealized account was of small comfort to Baptists. It glossed over the disabilities and harassments which made "friendly cohabitation" difficult for those who existed on the periphery of privilege. It did serve, on the other hand, to confirm representatives of the Standing Order in their view that they were pursuing an enlightened and benevolent policy of religious liberty. Those on the periphery of privilege, however, found Stiles's description of their situation far from persuasive. Small wonder that they should have greeted with some reserve John Adams's ringing summons in 1765 to join the Congregationalists in preaching up the doctrines and sentiments of religious liberty. Whose liberty did he have in mind?

II

With this backward glance at the Baptists in the years prior to 1770, the question still remains: How does one account for the emergence of the Baptists from relative obscurity in 1770 to become by 1800 the largest religious group in America, with twice as many adherents as the next largest denomination? By 1770 Baptists were increasing in number, but the total was still modest.

One indispensable prerequisite to Baptist success was wholehearted support of the American Revolution. In 1770 this support could not have been taken for granted. While Baptists shared the grievances of other colonists and were predisposed to join the agitation which preceded the Declaration of Independence, New England Baptists were momentarily ambivalent about breaking the ties with the mother country. They hesitated because their fight for liberty had not been with the British but with the New England Congregationalists. The Standing Order in New England was their major antagonist, circumscribing their freedom by actions of parish majorities and by regulations of the General Court. Indeed, from time to time, Baptists had been able to appeal to Britain for protection against the denial of what Baptists regarded as their "charter rights." Were Baptists prepared to sacrifice this advantage? From which direction came the greatest threat to their liberties?

In 1770 Backus noted that many New Englanders who were loudest in their "cry of LIBERTY and against oppressors are at the same time violating the dearest of all rights, LIBERTY OF CONSCIENCE."[15] Three years later, writing on behalf of the Grievance Committee of the Warren Association, Backus acknowledged that "a general union" for "the preservation of our liberties" was of great importance. But, he asked, "how can such a union be expected so long as that dearest of all rights, equal liberty of conscience, is not allowed?" You who "inhabit the land to which our ancestors fled for liberty" complain "because you are taxed where you are not represented." May we not make the same complaint of you? "Is it not really so with us?"[16]

It did not take New England Baptists long to resolve their dilemma. They quickly concluded that the greater threat came from England and England's bishops. The answer to their dilemma was to campaign on two fronts—against Britain for civil liberty and against the Congregationalists for religious liberty. They would join their neighbors to counter the threat from abroad without relaxing their struggle to secure religious liberty at home.

"While the defence of the civil rights of America appeared [to us] a matter of great importance," reported Backus in 1784, "our religious liberties were by no means to be neglected; and [among us] the contest concerning each kept a pretty even pace throughout the war."[17]

Elsewhere in the colonies, except perhaps in Virginia, Baptists had no such quandary to resolve. Even where there was an establishment of religion, the infringement of civil and religious liberties came from the same source. The government of the king and the church of the king constituted a common foe, and few Baptists entertained qualms about joining the revolutionary struggle.[18] The Anglican religious establishments, moreover, were mostly paper establishments which quickly toppled and collapsed.[19] Only in Virginia did the Church of England have any strong indigenous support, and in Virginia the Baptists adopted the two-front strategy being pursued in New England. In Virginia, John Leland provided the conspicuous leadership in the two-pronged enterprise, carrying on the struggle for religious freedom during the war years as part of the revolutionary struggle itself.[20]

A second external circumstance effectively reduced the competition for members. If identification with the Revolutionary cause was a factor favorable to Baptist growth, Anglicans and Quakers suffered from the lack of such identification. Both groups were casualties of the Revolution.

The Church of England, stigmatized as the church of the royal officials, survived the war as a dwindling denomination. Its unpopularity had been augmented by the ardent Toryism of most of its clergy, especially those sent out by the Society for the Propagation of the Gospel. Moreover, the church itself was in disarray. Some members had defected; some had gone to England; and some had joined the exodus of United Loyalists to Canada. Even more damaging was the loss of clergy, with only a small portion remaining after the war. Dwindling flocks were thus left without shepherds. Only a single Anglican clergyman remained in Pennsylvania, and this was true also in North Carolina and Georgia. New Jersey, with four, fared somewhat better. Virginia fared best of all, but even in Virginia the number of Anglican clergy declined from ninety-one to twenty-eight, and there were no new men to take the place of those who had departed.

The Quakers, who had been scattered in not insignificant numbers throughout all the colonies, were equally torn and weakened by the war. The pacifism of the Society of Friends precipitated numerous defections, and few "fighting Quakers" resumed their former religious affiliation. Furthermore, in some quarters Quakerism was suspect because of its presumed association with Toryism.[21]

The third factor which helps explain the dramatic shift in the fortunes of the Baptists was the new aggressive leadership they had acquired by 1770 from the "Separate" Congregationalists. It was a leadership sufficiently vigorous and energetic to carry on their two-front campaign for "liberty, both civil and religious," without being diverted from their evangelistic efforts. They were as busy seeking to convict people of sin and to lead them to a conversion experience as they were preaching up the war. And while they were winning converts and lending support to the struggle for independence, they also were carrying on lobbying activities in New England, in Virginia, and at the sessions of the Continental Congress to forward the cause of religious liberty. All three endeavors were viewed as interrelated and constituting but a single cause.

This seeming superabundance of energy is only a partial explanation of the success of the Baptist preachers. Even more important as an explanation of their effectiveness are two related features of Baptist clerical leadership. It was drawn directly from the ranks of the laity, and during the period from 1770 to 1800, in marked contrast to other denominations, it was never in short supply.

A fourth circumstance favorable to Baptist growth was the general climate of opinion. No other denomination was more closely in tune with the popular mood. According to Edmund Burke, a "fierce spirit of liberty" was at the bottom of the uproar in the colonies over sugar and stamps, tea and taxes.[22] During the course of the war this "fierce spirit of liberty" was further intensified. "Don't tread on me" was one slogan among many which expressed the spirit of Americans who had become chary of any infringement of their individual rights. To a people fiercely devoted to liberty and highly individualistic in temper, Baptists had a built-in appeal.

The Baptist appeal was especially self-evident in the consistency of the Baptist commitment to religious liberty, a term to which even those opposed to the elimination of all special privilege had to give at least lip service. Anglicans, at this point, were burdened with the albatross of two hundred years of history. Congregationalists also were tainted with the onus of special privilege and religious taxation. The Presbyterian clergy in Virginia were ready to settle for a "general assessment" and were called to account on this score by Presbyterian laity from "the Valley." Quakers, by the end of the Revolution, were out of contention as a possible major denomination.

In an even broader sense, the Baptist emphasis on individual rights, lay control, and local autonomy typified the American spirit. The accepted doctrine that there be "no government without the consent of the governed" placed primary stress on individual consent. Representation was necessary to accomplish certain ends, but the strength of anti-federalist sentiment made it clear that direct participation in decision making in one's own locality was much to be preferred. This was the popular mood. It was highly individualistic and highly self-assertive.

Most denominations scrambled in one way or another to adjust and adapt to the prevailing temper of the people. The prospects of a reconstituted Church of England were none too bright, and it was recognized in 1785 that, if it was to have any chance of survival, its constitution must conform to the dictates of republican sentiment. In drafting the constitution for the newly christened Protestant Episcopal Church, care was taken to safeguard the rights of local lay vestries, to provide for lay representation at all levels in the life of the church, and to delegate no powers to a General Convention which could be handled by a local congregation. The authority of bishops was circumscribed, being almost wholly limited to ceremonial and pastoral functions.

Roman Catholics were no less cognizant of the coercion imposed by the American temper in the post-war years. The effect of the pervasive American spirit on Roman Catholics was explained by Archbishop Maréchal of Baltimore in 1818.

> The American people pursue with a most ardent love the civil liberty which they enjoy. For the principle of civil liberty is paramount with them, so that absolutely all the magistrates, from the highest to the lowest, are elected by popular vote. . . . Likewise all the Protestant sects . . . are governed by these same principles, and as a result they elect and dismiss their pastors at will. Catholics in turn, living in their midst, are evidently exposed to the danger of admitting the same principles of ecclesiastical government.[23]

Catholics not only had been exposed to the danger, but also many had succumbed to it. John Carroll, who was to be the first Roman Catholic bishop in the United States, had written in 1783 that "our religious system has undergone a revolution, if possible, more extraordinary than our political one." As part of this revolution, Carroll insisted that American Catholics had a right to choose their own bishop, one "in whose appointment Rome shall have no share." Carroll also was firm in acknowledging the right of the laity to participate in the selection of the priest who was to be their pastor.[24] Even Carroll, however, would have judged that members of the congregation at Norfolk carried the adjustment to American ways too far when they asserted that the bishop, according to the "civil liberties" guaranteed by the laws of Virginia, had no authority to interfere in the affairs of any congregation or in "any of their religious matters, whatever."[25]

Congregationalists could have made an easy adjustment to the prevailing climate of opinion. Instead they continued to profess that they found no contradiction between their practice and the popular mood, and they remained saddled with the anomalies of the Standing Order. Presbyterians, for their part, were somewhat immobilized in attempting to reconcile the authority of a General Assembly with assertions of local rights until a compromise was reached which provided a kind of localism by endowing presbyteries with certain rights not subject to appeal. The compromise had the disadvantage, in terms of adapting to the temper of the time, of sheltering the clergy within the presbytery and thus protecting them from being overridden by local congregations.

Baptists, on the other hand, needed to make no concessions to the popular mood. They typified it. Whatever centralized organization the Philadelphia Association had provided disintegrated with the rapid multiplication of churches and local associations both during and after the war. By the end of the war Baptist democracy was firmly wedded to the independence and lay control of the local church. Baptists were so closely in tune with the temper of the time that they had no difficulty in regarding themselves and being regarded by others as a truly American church. The popular mood fostered by the Revolution could not have been more favorable to Baptist growth.

How does one account for the phenomenal growth of the Baptists? They had given unqualified support to the Revolution. Competition had been reduced. They had an ample supply of aggressive leadership. They were closely in tune with the popular mood. Finally, Baptists had developed a sense of mission and destiny that was related not only to the gospel but also to the emerging nation.

Isaac Backus had carefully cultivated the conviction that the Baptists were the true heirs of the Pilgrim Fathers, called to reform the existing order in New England to bring it into accord with the founding principles of the first settlers. During the course of the war this sense of mission was broadened and deepened. Baptists began to view their fight against the Standing Order in New England and against the Anglican establishment in Virginia as the opening battle of the American Revolution. As the new nation emerged after the war, Baptists more and more came to identify their own struggle for liberty with the aspirations of the American people as a whole. Baptists had contended for a return to the founding principles of the Pilgrim Fathers, and these were the same principles which were to serve as the foundation of the new nation.

Ever since the Great Awakening, Baptists had believed themselves to be engaged in a great work of redemption, looking forward with eager anticipation to the time when righteousness would be exalted and the wolf and the lamb, the leopard and the kid, the lion and the calf would lie down together. But indispensable to this harmony with God and one another which constitutes the millennium is a free society in which equality prevails, the sources of antagonism are removed, and no restraint is placed on the spread of God's truth. This was the larger vision, an intermingling of concern for "liberty, both civil and religious," to speed the time of reconciliation and purely voluntary obedience. This vision was the ground of the Baptists' vigorous evangelistic activity, and so attuned to the Revolutionary ethos had they become that their numbers multiplied with astonishing rapidity. As the most thoroughly "American" of all religious groups, it is not surprising that by 1800 Baptists had become the largest religious denomination in America.

NOTES

[1]Leonard Woolsey Bacon, *A History of American Christianity* (London: James Clarke & Co., 1899), p. 213. Lyman Beecher, "The Practicality of Suppressing Vice" in *Lyman Beecher and the Reform of Society* (New York: Arno Press, 1972), p. 19.

[2]Edwin S. Gaustad, *Historical Atlas of Religion in America* (New York: Harper & Row, Publishers, 1962), p. 52. Baptist numerical predominance was not to be challenged until some twenty years later when the Methodist Church, organized in 1784, had accumulated a full head of steam.

[3]A third point of contention was the practice of itinerant and lay preaching.

[4]William G. McLoughlin, *New England Dissent, 1630-1833*, 2 vols. (Cambridge, Mass.: Harvard University Press, 1971), vol. 1, p. 337.

[5]A similar division among Presbyterians did not produce the same result, for neither party among the Presbyterians was legally subordinated to and harassed by

the other. Neither Presbyterian group had to contend with the problem posed by a legal establishment and the intervention of governmental authority.

[6]William G. McLoughlin, *Isaac Backus and the American Pietistic Tradition*, ed. Oscar Handlin (Boston: Little, Brown and Company, 1967), p. 84.

[7]McLoughlin, *New England Dissent*, vol. 1, p. 491.

[8]Backus, *An Appeal to the Public* (1773), reprinted in William G. McLoughlin, ed., *Isaac Backus on Church, State, and Calvinism: Pamphlets 1754–1789* (Cambridge, Mass.: Harvard University Press, 1968), p. 339. Almost a quarter century earlier, Backus had initiated this theme when he wrote of "our fore Fathers who left their Pleasant Native Land for an houlling Wilderness . . . that they might have Liberty of Consciance." McLoughlin, *Isaac Backus and the American Pietistic Tradition*, p. 56. See also *ibid.*, p. 19.

[9]Isaac Backus, *A History of New England, with Particular Reference to the Denomination of Christians Called Baptists*, 2 vols. (Newton, Mass.: Backus Historical Society, 1871), vol. 1, p. 36.

[10]*Ibid.*, p. 37.

[11]Backus published the first volume of his *History of New England* in 1777.

[12]Backus, *History of New England*, vol. 1, p. viii; vol. 2, pp. 184-185.

[13]C. F. Adams, ed., *The Works of John Adams*, 10 vols. (New York: AMS Press, Inc., 1971), vol. 3, pp. 462, 464.

[14]Ezra Stiles, *A Discourse on the Christian Union* (Boston: Edes and Gill, 1761), pp. 37, 43, 97-99.

[15]McLoughlin, *Isaac Backus and the American Pietistic Tradition*, p. 122.

[16]McLoughlin, ed., *Isaac Backus on Church, State, and Calvinism*, pp. 338-339.

[17]McLoughlin, *Isaac Backus and the American Pietistic Tradition*, p. 135.

[18]Morgan Edwards in Philadelphia was a notable exception and was censured for his supposed Tory sympathies.

[19]This was true in New York, Maryland, North Carolina, South Carolina, and Georgia when the supporting prop of English authority was withdrawn. Typical was New York's speedy action in repealing all laws or acts which "may be construed to establish or maintain any particular denomination of Christians." The North Carolina Assembly anticipated the repudiation of British authority when it refused in 1773 to renew the Vestry Act. This had the practical effect of putting an end to the establishment.

[20]As early as June 12, 1776, Edmund Pendleton sought to forestall popular sentiment for religious liberty and to preserve some remnant of Virginia's religious establishment by securing the adoption of a "Declaration of Rights" which asserted that "all men are equally entitled to the free exercise of religion" but left untouched existing legislation of privilege and support. Later a "general assessment" to be distributed impartially among all Christian churches was proposed as a rear guard action in defense of the establishment. The issue was settled in 1785 with the adoption of the "Bill for Establishing Religious Freedom" which rejected any general assessment for religious purposes as well as any religious test for public office.

[21]Even Congregationalists suffered to some degree from the exodus of United Empire Loyalists.

[22]F. G. Selby, ed., *Burke's Speech on Conciliation with America* (London, 1912), pp. 17-21.

[23]John T. Ellis, ed., *Documents of American Catholic History* (Chicago: Henry Regnery Company, 1967), p. 214.

[24]James Hennesy, "Square Peg in a Round Hole," *Records of the American Catholic Historical Society of Philadelphia*, vol. 84 (December, 1973), pp. 170-171.

[25]*Documents of American Catholic History*, p. 221.

5
Stumbling
into Disorder

Chaotic may be too strong a word to use in describing the denominational structure of the Baptists, but there are few who will deny that there is confusion and disorder. Some sort of reorganization is necessary if Baptists are to make an effective witness in the critical age in which we live. Since a major obstacle to any attempt to make some sense of our denominational relationships is the rather widespread belief that the present structure is in some way derived from New Testament precepts or at least from historic Baptist principles, it is important to point out that this is *not* true. Our denominational structure has not been the product of biblical, theological, or even rational considerations. It was developed on an *ad hoc* basis as an efficient money-raising technique and to serve certain sectional and partisan concerns. The story is complicated, but it is filled with human interest. To tell it should serve to free us from some of the preconceptions which hinder us from reorganizing our denominational life.

I

There were not many Baptist churches in America prior to the American Revolution—only ten in Pennsylvania, for example, and twenty in New Jersey. These churches were linked together more or less effectively in the Philadelphia Baptist Association. Toward the close of the colonial period some marked growth had taken place in New England, Virginia, and the Carolinas, and the denominational pattern was modified to permit churches in these areas to be represented in the Philadelphia Association through subsidiary Associations rather than by delegates from each church. During the war the number of Baptists continued to increase, and by the time it was over the old plan of union had broken down completely.

Various proposals were made for linking the new local Associations which were springing up everywhere once again in a national organization, but none of them received widespread support. This was largely because the Philadelphia Association, by herculean efforts, continued to assume many of the responsibilities which should have been shouldered by the denomination as a whole, and the other Associations, preoccupied with their own immediate concerns, were quite content to let the Philadelphia Association do this for them. It was not until Luther Rice returned to America to enlist the support of Baptists for Adoniram Judson's pioneering missionary venture in Burma that the problem posed by the absence of any national organization became acute.

Numerous observers of our social history have pointed out that the characteristic response of an Englishman or American, when confronted by an immediately urgent need, has always been to form a committee or society and to get on with the job. It is not surprising, therefore, that Luther Rice should have adopted this traditional method of organization to meet a specific need. This was a means of achieving quick action by interested people, but was not intended to provide a denominational structure. As a result of the efforts of Luther Rice, the General Convention of the Baptist Denomination in the United States for Foreign Missions (more commonly known as the Triennial Convention since it met every three years) was formed in 1814.

From its beginning the Triennial Convention had other responsibilities than foreign missions thrust upon it. It was almost inevitable that it should become concerned with home as well as with foreign missions, for success in the foreign field was dependent upon a strong base of support at home. Indispensable to both was trained leadership. By the time of its second meeting in 1817, the larger responsibility of the Triennial Convention for education, as well as for home and foreign missions, was explicitly acknowledged by an amendment to the constitution, and in 1820 the phrase "and other important objects relating to the Redeemer's kingdom" was added to the official title of the Convention.

The Triennial Convention, as a voluntary society, was a temporary expedient, and it was widely recognized that a more formal connection between the churches was essential. The plan that gradually evolved was to extend the associational principle by bringing Associations together in State Conventions, and then linking the State Conventions in a genuine General Convention of the churches. As individual churches sent delegates to Associations to deal with their common concerns, so the various Associations could send delegates to a State Convention with the same object in view. The State Conventions could then send delegates to a General Convention, thus uniting the churches of the whole country.

The first step was the organization of State Conventions on this model. By 1820 there were more than eighteen Associations in New York alone, and at least seventeen in Virginia. Acting independently these Associations often provided a superabundance of missionary effort in certain areas, while other fields equally needy were neglected. Furthermore, the educational funds at the disposal of any one Association were too limited to do more than help defray the expenses of students at some non-Baptist academy, college, or seminary. The first State Conventions formed of delegates from the Associations were organized in 1821 in South Carolina and New York. Two years later similar bodies were formed in Georgia and Alabama; in 1824 Maine, Vermont, Massachusetts, Virginia, and Mississippi took the same step; and Rhode Island, New Hampshire, and Ohio followed suit shortly thereafter.

In Boston the editors of the *American Baptist Magazine* reported the South Carolina action with unconcealed enthusiasm.

> We cannot but remark that our brethren in the South have in this as in so many other cases presented us an example most worthy of imitation. We have long been sensible of the want of some such organization as this for every state in the Union. ... Our Associations unite our churches; why should not a Convention unite our Associations?[1]

The *American Baptist Magazine* and its editor Francis Wayland were equally enthusiastic in advocating the formation of a General Convention composed of delegates from the State Convention. The Massachusetts Convention incorporated a provision in its constitution which stated that "whenever a General Convention formed from State Conventions throughout the United States shall be formed or designed, it shall be in the power of this Convention to send delegates to meet in such Convention."[2]

The culmination of the movement came in 1826. The Triennial Convention of 1823 had urged the formation of State Conventions, and as the 1826 meeting approached Luther Rice suggested that the time had come to transform the Triennial Convention into a genuine General Convention composed of delegates from the State Convention which had been formed in almost every state. He pointed out that under the existing system delegates were appointed by local missionary and educational societies which contributed to its funds. This had led to unequal representation.

> The funds of almost any individual society are small, and to send a delegate from a remote state would frequently exhaust its whole contributions for the year. Thus from remote states it could scarcely be expected that any, or at most but one or two, delegates would be present, and these would represent a society of 25 or 30 individuals instead of the whole state from which they come.

The practical effect of this provision, he noted, could be seen in the last Convention when more delegates were present from the city of Washington than from the whole of New England. Such an arrangement meant that policy would always be determined by a small group of men rather than by the "united wisdom of our brethren." On the other hand, if the members of the Convention were appointed by the State Conventions, "a more general attendance might be expected," for a State Convention "could always bear, with trifling exertion, the expenses of its delegation." Furthermore, those who would attend on this basis would represent not simply their own personal point of view or that of a small local society but would voice the feelings of the total Baptist constituency in their state.[3]

There does not seem to have been much opposition to the proposed Convention structure, and in all areas of the denomination it had found warm support. The *New York Baptist Register* had been one of its early advocates; Francis Wayland had written in 1824 one of the most persuasive statements of the logic of taking this step; and state after state had proceeded to adopt this extension of the associational principle by organizing State Conventions. From all published evidence, everyone seems to have expected equally expeditious action to complete the structure with a General Convention composed of representatives from the State Conventions. Actually, the proposal never came before the Convention of 1826, for the delegates who were present proceeded to dismantle the existing Convention instead. The surprising feature of this strange turn of events is that the dismembering operation was carried out by delegates from Massachusetts and New York who had been among the strongest advocates of the Convention structure.

Apparently Luther Rice feared that some maneuver to seize control of the Convention was afoot; for just a month before the

Convention met, he pointed out that the existing arrangement could easily be abused by an "active and intriguing man." "I hope," he wrote, "the time will never arrive when any man among us will be disposed to intrigue in the cause of Christ, but still it will not be doubted that leaving the possibility of such an event open is an objection to any arrangement, which it would be wise in us to obviate if it be in our power."[4]

II

The shape of things to come had been foreshadowed in New York. A State Convention, composed of delegates from the Associations, had been formed in 1821. A missionary society of more than local significance, however, had been in existence since 1807. This was the Hamilton Baptist Missionary Society, which found its leadership and much of its support in the Madison Association but carried on extensive missionary activities throughout the state. Because of this duplication of effort, the State Convention proposed in 1824 that the Hamilton Missionary Society unite with the State Convention. After lengthy negotiations and delay in publishing of the proceedings, the union was finally consummated early in 1825. However, instead of the Hamilton Society uniting with the State Convention as had been expected, the State Convention joined the Hamilton Missionary Society. The Society retained its own constitution but changed its name to the Baptist Missionary Convention of the State of New York.

How this reversal of the original intention was brought about is not entirely clear, but the basic considerations determining the outcome are evident enough. On the eve of the negotiations, the *Register,* which was the organ of the Convention, was urging that similar Conventions composed of delegates from Associations be formed in every state and that delegates from these Conventions should constitute the national Convention.[5] The point of view of the Hamilton Missionary Society was later expressed in the report of the committee it had appointed to carry on the negotiations. Your committee, it stated,

> did not for a moment lose sight of those plain practical principles incorporated in the constitution of this Society under which for seventeen years we have so happily, unitedly, and successfully rallied. The committee saw no reason to abandon those principles, although they desired an increase of influence and usefulness which union with their brethren was calculated to effect.

After what the committee of the Society reported as "suitable deliberation," the committee of the Convention "agreed to recommend to that body the adoption of the constitution of this Society."[6]

The publicized reason for shifting from a body composed of delegates from the various Associations to a body composed of individuals who contributed to its funds was the superior utility of the latter as a money-raising technique. The Hamilton Society had been eminently successful in making full use of this method, and the plan was now to have every Association resolve itself into an auxiliary society and every church form itself into a branch society of the auxiliary. In addition, female societies, youth societies, and children's societies could be formed. Since membership in each society would be based on dues in the form of contributions, the immediate advantage in raising money was clearly apparent.

One suspects that, in addition to this practical consideration, there were also other, less publicized reasons for the shift. The Madison Association had developed a wealth of leadership in the various benevolent societies it had fostered, but under the associational plan of representation only a few of these men could be sent as delegates to the State Convention. While they had complete control of the Hamilton Society, the Madison Association would only be entitled to send five, out of a possible one hundred delegates to the State Convention. Their influence would be drastically reduced. One can easily understand, therefore, the tenacity with which the men from the Madison Association clung to the arrangement embodied in the constitution of the Hamilton Society, for it permitted them to retain control of its operations.

Apparently a bargain was made with the Convention committee. The Society would adopt the name of the Convention while retaining its own constitution. The membership of the Board of the Society would be increased to thirty so that it could include the members of the State Convention's negotiating committee as well as twelve men from the Madison Association. Three other concessions had to be made in order to secure the merger on the basis of transforming the Convention into a voluntary society. The *Western Baptist Magazine* of the Hamilton Society was to be discontinued in favor of the Convention's *Register;* the two editors of the *Register* were to be the president and the secretary of the newly reconstituted Convention; and the headquarters of the Convention was to be at Utica rather than at Hamilton.

One other consideration also seems to have been involved in

the negotiations. The newly reorganized Convention was to be restricted solely to missionary concerns, and its name was altered to make this fact clear. It was to be the Baptist *Missionary* Convention of the State of New York, and the specific concern excluded was education. The Baptist Education Society of the State of New York had been founded at Hamilton in 1817 by the same men who conducted the affairs of the Hamilton Missionary Society, and in 1820 the seminary of the Education Society had opened its doors at Hamilton and held its first classes. One can well imagine that these men who had invested so heavily in the infant institution did not wish their control of the seminary to be disturbed, and as a consequence insisted that the State Convention should be excluded from the field of education.

A further step to safeguard their control of the seminary was soon taken. All who contributed to the Education Society became members of the Society and were entitled to vote at its annual meeting. Although few from any distance ever attended or could even be expected to attend, there was always the possibility that on some future occasion some members of the Board might be dislodged. Apparently to obviate this possibility, a new method of collecting funds was devised and put into operation in the same year that the Hamilton Society and the State Convention were united. An Association of Alumni and Friends was proposed by Professor Daniel Hascall as a means of raising money, and on December 23, 1825, such an organization was formed. There were practically no alumni since instruction had only begun in 1820, but throughout the churches there were many friends. These friends could now secure an annual membership in the Association by contributing ten dollars, and they became life members if they contributed fifty dollars at one time.[7] As members they were eligible to become officers of the Association, but their only function was to turn over the funds they collected to the Baptist Education Society of the State of New York, which retained control of the seminary in its hands.

III

When the Triennial Convention met, it was obvious that both New York and Massachusetts had made careful preparation for the Convention, for almost two-thirds of the delegates were from these two states. The *New York Baptist Register,* on March 24, had announced the forthcoming meeting and had urged that there be "a full assemblage of delegates," for "subjects of great import will unquestionably occupy the deliberations of this body." One week later, it reported that the Board of the State Convention was to meet at Utica "to take measures preparatory to the meeting of the General Convention on the 26th day of April next. A punctual attendance is earnestly requested." The following week, on April 7, the *Register* reported that the Board of the State Convention at its Utica meeting had appointed a committee of ten "in behalf of said body to confer with the Baptist General Convention at their sitting in New York . . . on subjects connected with the interests of the State Convention." Steps were immediately taken to have the members of the State Convention committee appointed as delegates from local missionary societies. As a result of such efforts, it is not surprising that there was a large New York delegation on hand when the General Convention convened for its 1826 meeting. Of the sixty-eight delegates present, twenty-two were from New York and seventeen were from Massachusetts. On April 25, the *Register* commented: "We are persuaded that there will be much talent in this Convention." No meeting of the Convention, it observed, "was ever so full of interest."

This preparation was the product of discontent in Massachusetts as well as in New York. Massachusetts was the strongest center of interest in foreign missions and its most generous source of support. This was understandable, for ships regularly sailed to the Far Pacific, from Salem and Boston, bringing back with them news of the strange lands of the Orient. Massachusetts Baptists, therefore, were more dismayed than others by the fact that since 1820 the funds collected by the Triennial Convention for foreign missions had been declining. The transplanted Yankees of New York, because of their close ties with New England, may also have been somewhat more disturbed than Baptists in other sections of the country by this decline in foreign mission income.

At the Convention of 1823, there had been a strong feeling among the Massachusetts delegates that the cause of foreign missions had suffered because of the Convention's interest in Columbian College, which it had established in 1820 in Washington, D.C. Feeling ran so high that Luther Rice was specifically charged with misappropriating funds, a charge from which he was completely exonerated. Still the feeling persisted, and a year later the *New York Baptist Register* announced that "it has long been known that the numerous avocations and especially the pressing calls of the Columbian College have so occupied the attention of our dear brethren at Washington that the cause of

Foreign Missions has not received the attention which its importance demanded."[8]

Luther Rice, to be sure, had been devoting much of his time to Columbian College, for it was his firm conviction that the college was indispensable to the success of both home and foreign missions. And since he received the whole of his compensation from the college, he did not believe that his activity in its behalf was open to serious criticism. His services to the Convention were wholly voluntary. But in order to put an end to the continuing criticism, the Board of the Convention adopted a plan in 1824 whereby the immediate responsibility for promoting foreign mission interest would be assigned to the Committee on Outfit in and about Boston. This committee was authorized to employ such agents as it deemed necessary for the purpose of soliciting funds, to recommend candidates for missionary appointment, to supervise the disbursement of foreign mission funds, and to nominate a person who would be appointed Assistant Corresponding Secretary to carry on correspondence with missionaries. Finally, so that there might be no further question with regard to the handling of funds, the Boston committee was asked to nominate one of their own number to be appointed Treasurer of the Convention.

Actually, the decline in giving had not been the fault either of Luther Rice or of the Convention. It was a consequence of the depression which set in with the Western Panic of 1819 and continued its downward spiral until 1824. Credit had been overextended to the land speculators, the wildcat banks had collapsed, and in many areas of the country money was practically nonexistent. The end of the Napoleonic Wars also adversely affected the trade of the northern seaboard, and these states were beset by hard times.

The centering of the attack upon Columbian College suggests that the criticism was motivated quite as much by hostility to the College as it was by a concern for foreign missions. In New York the criticism was sparked by men who were closely identified with the theological seminary at Hamilton, and the financial needs of the seminary were urgent. In December, 1825, the accounts were already in arrears and a further debt was accumulating. The number of students was rapidly increasing, thus creating the problem of providing additional support. A new building was needed, and the library was reported to be completely inadequate.[9] In Massachusetts, the Massachusetts Baptist Education Society had been eager to establish a seminary in the vicinity of Boston. Francis

Wayland took the lead in the project, and instruction was begun in December, 1825.* Preoccupied as they were with their own educational ventures, the Baptist leaders of Massachusetts and New York tended to regard with something less than enthusiasm the prospect of participating in the sponsorship of a college and seminary at Washington, even though that institution had been designed to serve an urgent national denominational need and had been so located that it might serve Baptists from Pennsylvania and New Jersey to Georgia and over the mountains to Kentucky and Tennessee—a vast area in which no other Baptist college or seminary existed.

A third source of tension seems to have been the *Latter Day Luminary*, the official magazine of the Triennial Convention. The *American Baptist Magazine*, published by the Baptist Missionary Society of Massachusetts, had also, on its own initiative, undertaken to publicize the work of the Convention. When responsibility for foreign missions was largely delegated to the Committee on Outfit in Boston, it was expressly stated that "all intelligence received from our missionaries of a character suitable for publication shall be communicated to the editors of the *American Baptist Magazine* and the *Latter Day Luminary*."[10]

Francis Wayland was editor of the *American Baptist Magazine*, and there is some evidence to indicate that he thought his journal alone should represent the foreign mission interest now that the scene of operations had been shifted to Boston. Less than a year before he had preached the annual sermon before the Boston Baptist Foreign Mission Society on the theme "The Moral Dignity of the Missionary Enterprise." When it was published two months later, the sermon was greeted with nationwide acclaim, a fact which Wayland confessed may have caused him to place a "high estimate" on his own abilities and which certainly led him to regard himself as the major spokesman for foreign missions. In any event, the next issue of the *American Baptist Magazine* carried the following curious announcement:

> We shall not consider ourselves bound . . . to publish every article, which might otherwise be thought suitable for the Magazine, if sent

---

*It is interesting to note that the seminary was officially divorced from the Massachusetts Baptist Education Society and control was vested in a self-perpetuating board of trustees, of which Wayland was secretary. The Education Society, however, retained responsibility for raising the necessary money to purchase a plot of land in Newton, erect buildings, and underwrite the operating expenses of the institution.

first for insertion in some other paper. . . . It is not our intention in the slightest degree to interfere with the claims of any other religious publication, but we certainly feel it a duty which we owe the Society to employ all prudent means to preserve and increase the prosperity and usefulness of our own.[11]

The "any other religious publication" most likely refers to the *Latter Day Luminary,* toward which Wayland manifested a persistent hostility.

A fourth source of tension was also present. The "era of good feeling" had come to an end. Everywhere in New England men were beginning to discuss the threat posed by the expanding West. It was suddenly dawning upon them that the West would soon become a dominant influence and power in national life. This the New Englanders and their Yankee cousins in New York could only regard as a disaster, for it could mean victory for the "barbarism" of the frontier and the subversion of the moral order of society so well exemplified in the life and institutions of the New England communities. One response to this challenge was to be a redoubling of home missionary activity in the western territory; a more immediate response was to cling more tightly to whatever controls the New Englanders already possessed.

IV

The fight to dismember the Triennial Convention in 1826 was led by Francis Wayland. Baron Stow, who was present, has reported: "In the various discussions, some of which were profoundly exciting, Mr. Wayland earnestly participated, and by his cool, conclusive reasonings, contributed largely to the wise results which were ultimately reached. . . . In fact, he did more than any other man to secure the separation of the college from the Convention."[12] Wayland acknowledged that although he was somewhat of a failure as a pastor, he was able to get things done. "I am built railroad fashion," he was to say later. "I can go forward if necessary, and if necessary I can take the back track—but I cannot go sideways."[13] On this occasion he was determined to go forward.

What probably triggered the struggle into which Way-land threw himself was Luther Rice's suggestion that the time had come to transform the Triennial Convention into a genuine General Convention of the whole denomination. This was, of course, what Wayland himself had been advocating only a short time before.[14] But now it must have occurred to him, as it had occurred to the men of the Hamilton Missionary Society, that to have men sent as delegates by State Conventions, in place of the spotty representation from local societies, would provide a balanced body in which the influence and power of those who had previously been most active in denominational life would be sharply reduced.

Rice also was proposing that responsibility for foreign missions be centered in one place. He had noted the confusion and inefficiency created by the attempt to operate the affairs of the Convention from two centers—Washington and Boston. While the Boston group had been given complete freedom to hire agents and raise money, it had been intended that the appointment of missionaries and the actual appropriation of funds would come before the Board in Washington in the form of recommendations. However, the Boston group instead of referring to itself as a Standing Committee had tended to style itself the Baptist Board of Foreign Missions and proceeded to act quite independently of the Board of the Convention. Rice's proposal to centralize responsibility could only mean one thing to the Boston group, a serious curtailment of the almost unlimited authority actually being exercised by the Committee on Outfit.[15]

When the Convention met on April 26, 1826, the Massachusetts and New York delegates were apparently determined to accomplish three major goals—to separate Columbian College from the Convention, to retain control of foreign missions in Boston, and to sidetrack the proposal to have the Convention composed of delegates from State Conventions. The last was especially important, for in a Convention formed on this basis they would lose the predominance which they had managed to secure in this particular assembly.

Although they already had sufficient votes to carry the day, it was necessary to move cautiously if so radical a shift from the prevailing sentiment for a General Convention was to be effected without completely disrupting the denomination. The strategy they had devised involved a two-pronged attack. The first objective was to discredit Rice and thus to destroy the effectiveness of his leadership and demoralize the opposition. The second objective was to present an alternative to a General Convention that could be defended with convincing and persuasive arguments.

It is difficult to believe that any group of Christians could have set out in cold blood to blacken the reputation of one of their colleagues, but it is equally difficult to read the evidence concerning the attack upon Rice and reach any other conclusion.

We shall remember, of course, that the men who led the attack were deeply concerned for the success of the missionary enterprises in which they were involved. They were firmly convinced that they possessed the necessary experience, wisdom, and ability to assure the desired results, if only the direction of affairs were left in their hands. And Luther Rice, with his prestige and influence, constituted the great obstacle to their plans. In addition, antagonisms and animosities had been generating over a period of time, and feeling was now running high. Under these circumstances, people always have difficulty distinguishing between honest judgment and party passion.

During the first week of the Convention delaying tactics were adopted. Routine business was transacted, but many important matters—including the report of the Agent and the report of the Board of Managers—were laid on the table. Rice's name had been excluded from the nominations for trustees of Columbian College. This occasioned considerable controversy, but discussion of this issue was persistently postponed. The purpose of the delay was to wait for committee reports; and the committees were obviously engaged in behind-the-scenes maneuvers. The usual committees had been appointed, most of them heavily loaded with New Englanders and New Yorkers. Their primary objective, judging by their reports, seems to have been to get something on Rice. In addition, a special committee "On the Conduct of Mr. Rice" had been appointed, at his suggestion, in an effort to clear his name.

It was not until the eighth day of the Convention—the day on which the Convention had been scheduled to adjourn—that the delegates finally got down to business. The committee on the *Latter Day Luminary* (headed by Francis Wayland) presented a negative report stating that no ledger had been kept by which the accounts might be balanced, since the subscriptions had been entered in a subscription book and the receipts were scattered through a daily journal. The report insinuated that there was grave cause for alarm. This was a picayune objection, for the *Latter Day Luminary* was a minor enterprise, conducted on a part-time, volunteer basis. The major portion of the cost of the printing equipment and the building which housed it had been contributed by Rice out of his own personal funds. Nevertheless, the report was received and the whole matter referred to the Board for appropriate action. The following day the committee on the Agent's Accounts reported that they had found nothing erroneous in them *"since the last Convention."* The qualifying phrase was emphasized in the printed report by being put in italics. Actually, of course, the committee was charged only with examining Rice's accounts since the last Convention, and at the last Convention they had been found in order.

On May 5, the committee "On the Conduct of Mr. Rice" reported. Lucius Bolles, who was to succeed Rice as the executive officer of the Board, was chairman. Their report was a strange document. The committee had "found it difficult to fix upon particular facts upon which to place a censure," yet there had been indiscretions and mistakes in judgment. It was felt that Rice should be held personally responsible for decisions that had the sanction of the Board—a twist of logic which permitted the conclusion that he had abused the high confidence that had been placed in him. Although they had found nothing definitely censurable, the committee expressed the hope that "a sense of past indiscretions may render him more wise in the future." The sum of his guilt was two-fold. He had displayed initiative and enterprise in carrying out the directives of the Convention and the Board, qualities not conspicuous by their absence among his accusers; and he had made two investments which had not proved entirely profitable because of the deepening economic depression. The report having been made, the Convention proceeded to adopt a resolution of censure.

With Rice discredited, the New York and Massachusetts delegations were firmly in control. They then proceeded to dissolve the connection with Columbian College and voted to locate the headquarters of the Board in Boston. It was not until the Committee on Amendments to the Constitution reported on Monday, May 8, that it was possible to complete the objectives of their program. A motion was then in order to dismiss the committee and appoint Jonathan Going of Massachusetts, Spencer H. Cone of New York, and Elon Galusha of New York as a new committee to propose further alterations to the constitution. The major alteration proposed by this committee and adopted at the afternoon session was to restrict the Convention to the foreign mission interest.

V

It is a maxim of politics that you cannot beat somebody with nobody, and the same truth applies to a proposed program of action which has widespread support. An alternative program must be offered in its stead. The alternative to the State and

National Convention denominational structure which had gained so much momentum had been put forward by the New York convention in the *Register* for October 19, 1825.

> We are happy to observe by the result of actual experiment that the plan recommended in the last address of the Convention for Associations to resolve themselves into missionary societies auxiliary to the Convention, and the churches to resolve themselves into branch societies . . . has been productive of the most heart cheering encouragement. And your Board are confirmed in the opinion that this system . . . possesses decided advantage over every other yet proposed. This promises eventually to bring the great body of the denomination into one missionary society which shall acquire a stability and permanency far beyond anything that can rationally be expected from any other plan hitherto projected.

Among the features of the New York plan had been the exclusion of the educational interest, and this was admirably suited to any plan to divorce Columbian College from the Triennial Convention. However, one further modification was needed to meet the desire of the Boston group to retain control of the foreign mission enterprise. If the home and foreign mission interests were also separated, a strong case could be made for locating the headquarters of the foreign board in Boston, because trade with the Orient was carried on from the New England ports. This was the plan adopted, and the printed report of the 1826 Convention summarized the alterations that had been made by saying that the Convention "is now a simple body, with one undivided object, and that object is the promulgation of the gospel among the heathen."

Three major arguments were developed to support this individual society plan of operation—none of them involving an appeal to biblical precept, theological doctrine, or historic Baptist principle. First, it was contended that there is no necessary connection between the different benevolent objects and thus no reason why they should be united in one body. Second, there is an actual disadvantage in having them managed by the same men; for when this is the case, the different objects will not be pursued with the same vigor and one will suffer at the expense of another. Third, the society system is much more efficient and effective in raising money. Not only does the membership feature have decided advantages, but also the division of objects among different societies. "Some [people] are more particularly favorable to missionary and others to educational exertions. The blending of these two concerns together must evidently injure the success of both of them. . . . Either party would give more liberally towards his favorite object if it stood alone and totally disconnected with the other."[16]

The first argument, that there was no necessary connection between the various benevolent objects, completely revised what had previously been contended. Until this time, all agreed that home and foreign missions and educational endeavors were intimately interrelated and that, without an assignment of general responsibility, some areas of concern might be neglected by oversight and not receive the attention they deserved.

The second argument, that the same men could not effectively direct different objects, was even more startling. The very men who set forth this argument were themselves responsible for a multitude of different causes in their own areas. Francis Wayland, for example, who was now to become recording secretary of what remained of the Triennial Convention, was already secretary of the Baptist Convention of Massachusetts, the Boston Baptist Foreign Mission Society, and the Newton Board of Trustees. He was also a member of the boards of managers of the Baptist Missionary Society of Massachusetts, the Baptist Education Society of Massachusetts, and the Evangelical Tract Society. Furthermore, he was a member of the Standing Committee in and about Boston of the Triennial Convention, and editor of the *American Baptist Magazine,* which was able to promote all the different benevolent objects with impartiality. Wayland was not a unique figure in this respect. Actually, all the offices of the various societies and boards in Massachusetts were held by about a dozen men. In New York and elsewhere, the situation was the same.

The third argument was the most plausible and persuasive. But the benefits to be derived from a separation of the different appeals were undoubtedly overstated. Everywhere one turns during this period, the same people are found to have been interested in all the benevolent objects. If a person was interested in missions, he would almost certainly also be interested in education; and if he contributed to these two causes, he was also probably contributing to the Bible, tract, and Sunday School societies. The new system, however, was to prove far from efficient and effective. Without centralization all the various causes were compelled to engage in free-lance operations, and a horde of agents soliciting funds descended on the churches. For more than a century, the churches · in the North were to be bedeviled by this problem, and the denomination was to engage in endless negotiations in an attempt to bring some order out of the chaos. In the South the churches were to be spared much of this problem; for when the Southern Baptist Convention was organized, the constitution of the Triennial Convention, without the troublesome amendments of 1826, was adopted.

VI

In the North improvisations in the denominational structure did not end with the Convention of 1826. Nineteen years later the slavery controversy led to a division between the Baptists of the North and the South. In 1845, when Francis Wayland was serving as president of what remained of the Triennial Convention, a special meeting of the Board was held on September 24 and 25 to consider the problems created by the withdrawal of the Baptists in the South from the Convention. Wayland, among others, saw in this crisis an opportunity to reshape the structure of the denomination once again. A special meeting of the Convention was deemed to be necessary, and a committee, of which Wayland was a member, recommended that the special Convention consider not only the problem created by the formation of a new "missionary organization at the South and the new relations thence arising" but also "the imperfections in the provisions of our present constitution." A committee of eight—three from Boston, four from New York City, and Wayland from Providence—was appointed to recommend such alterations in the constitution as might be thought necessary.

When the special Convention met in New York City on November 19, the committee did not recommend alterations to the constitution. Instead, they proposed, in effect, that the Convention be dissolved and be replaced by an American Baptist Foreign Missionary Union with an entirely new constitution. The basic difference would be in the definition of membership. Formerly the Convention had been composed of *delegates* of those bodies—whether missionary societies, Associations, or churches—which contributed to its funds; the new Union was to be composed of *individuals* who became life members of the Union by virtue of their presence as delegates at the present session or in the future by contributing one hundred dollars at one time to the Union. The new constitution was adopted "as merely prospective and conditional," since it would be necessary to secure acts of the legislatures in both Pennsylvania and Massachusetts before its final adoption. The Convention, thereupon, recessed to reassemble again on May 19, 1846, to complete the reorganization.

At the adjourned meeting in May, the first action was to accept the acts which had been adopted by the Pennsylvania and Massachusetts legislatures. This may have been a clever parliamentary device, for the next resolution was to proceed with the election of officers, since the acts of the two legislatures had been predicated upon "a certain constitution, at such time conditionally adopted. . . , [becoming] unconditional and definitive on the procural of certain legislative acts." The constitution had thus come into effect without any further discussion, debate, or vote. Alfred Bennett, who as a traveling agent of the Convention and now of the Union was sensitive to the feelings of people in the churches, immediately protested the aristocratic character of the new organization, and proposed that churches which contributed one hundred dollars during the year should be permitted to represent themselves in the Union by annual members. This proposal was quickly sidetracked by referring it to the Board for consideration in accordance with the provision of the new constitution.

The interesting feature of the new constitution was the concentration of power in the hands of the few. Membership, of course, was restricted to life members who had paid at one time what was then a considerable sum of money. But the following provisions were also significant: a special meeting of the Union could be called only by the Board, and a special meeting of the Board could be called only by the Executive Committee; the Executive Committee was given authority to appoint all missionaries and all agents and to fix their compensation, to make all appropriations, and to remove any corresponding secretary, treasurer, auditing committee, or missionary, and to appoint others in their places; and amendments to the constitution could be made *"only upon recommendation by the Board of Managers,"* and at an annual meeting by a vote of two-thirds of those present. Life members, having purchased their own membership, could scarcely be anticipated to be in any mood to relax the requirements for membership and thus undercut their own position in the Union. Nor could any large number of the life members, no longer being in a position to have their expenses paid by somebody, ever be expected to attend the annual meeting. Thus, control by headquarters—a small group of the wisest and most experienced friends of foreign missions—seemed assured.

Alfred Bennett's proposal received no attention at the first meeting of the Board of the new American Baptist Missionary Union. A year later, at the Union's annual meeting in Cincinnati, the Board reported that it had decided to postpone any discussion of the subject at that time because many of the members, including two-thirds of the Board, could not be present. Therefore, they said, it was taken "for granted that the comparatively small number who are present will hardly wish to decide a question of such magnitude, involving a fundamental principle of our organization and associated with interests of the gravest character, which must be jeopardized and may be seriously damaged by a hasty decision."

It is difficult to tell how widespread was the opposition to the new constitutional provisions, but a year later proponents of the new system admitted that opposition was vigorous and that formal action had been taken against it by the churches in Maine, Connecticut, western New York, Ohio, and Michigan. Quite obviously the Board could not ride out the storm by ignoring the issue. The usual resort in such a situation was adopted, and a "Committee of Nine on the Alteration of the Constitution" was appointed to make a thorough study of the question. A year later, in 1848, the committee had its report ready, but the Board informed the annual meeting of the Union that discussion would be postponed for still another year, and that prior to the next annual meeting the report of the committee would be mailed to each member of the Union, together with a covering letter to be drafted by Francis Wayland, requesting an expression of opinion on the question.

VII

The eighteen-page report of the Committee of Nine[17] was a full-blown apologetic for the new setup. It suggested that "the new instrument" was of "very recent adoption and deserves, before amendment, at least its full term of trial," and then, with what can only be described as Alice-in-Wonderland logic, it proceeded to deal with the various objections to it that had been raised.

"The imputation of aristocratic tendencies," the report contended, is to be "utterly denied." Actually, "the existing system is far more democratic and popular than the former." Under the new arrangement, for example, it costs only one hundred dollars for a man to become a member of the Union for life, whereas formerly it cost a church or another organization one hundred dollars each year to send an annual delegate to the Convention. Over a period of twenty years, it would cost such a body two thousand dollars to maintain one delegate at the annual sessions. Now, by utilizing its funds to purchase life memberships for individuals, a church could make twenty men life members for the same amount of money. "The old system as requiring the more money was essentially the more aristocratic." Furthermore, "the basis of local representation" is "widely broadened," and "the elective franchise in choosing our missionary boards is very greatly extended through the churches." Under the older law of membership the state of New Jersey had "an average of some ten delegates in your annual meetings, whereas now she has some thirty-five life members."

The flaws in this argument were two-fold. First, the comparison was between delegates who had attended the annual meetings and life members, of whom only a few could ever be expected to attend. Second, the life memberships were explicitly designed to avoid the principle of representation by giving a person permanent and independent tenure, so that he would feel no obligation to reflect the sentiments of his church. A person whose membership fee had been supplied by a church might soon thereafter arrive at convictions quite at variance with those of a majority of the members of the church; he might lose interest and drop out of the church; he might even be excluded—but he would still remain a life member of the Union and, in effect, represent no one but himself.

The report argued that the new system, in addition to being "more democratic," also avoided putting church membership on a *"moneyed basis."* Those who suggest that the church and the missionary society should be coextensive automatically exclude from the church "the converted pauper . . . , because like Lazarus he has only prayers and not coin to offer for his share in the membership . . . on a missionary platform." This makes *"gold* a platform where Christ made *grace* such." On the other hand, if an attempt is made to avoid this evil by adopting "the principle that every church member, poor or rich, is from his standing in the church a member of your missionary organization, how will you, then, shut out from the control of the missionary work the many Christians, and churches even, who as yet have shown no adequate interest in the work?" To have "the infant missionary enterprises of the day" placed indiscriminately under the control of those who have manifested neither a "peep" nor a "mutter" of sympathy for the heathen would be like giving "the lamb to be suckled by the she-wolf."

Some had suggested that the one hundred dollar life membership restricted control to the wealthy, and that the constitution should be modified to permit contributing churches ' to appoint annual members. This change, the report contended in its own brand of logic, would have just the reverse effect. This one amendment, if adopted, would give rise, year by year, to demands for further amendments involving ever more dangerous concessions. "These amendments, pleading the narrow means of some feebler churches, will sink yet lower the terms of admission until ten dollars even may constitute a member for the year." It would then be in "the power of any wealthier churches, having an object to be attained," to procure from these churches—by paying the necessary ten dollars—the appointment of an annual member amenable to their purposes. By this means wealthy churches could "flood" the meetings of the Union with "a large and local delegation of annual members, sweeping before their numbers and inexperience all opposition that might be attempted on the part of long missionary experience and true missionary ardor." Thus, the report argued that the new system was actually designed to serve as a safeguard against all efforts to place the churches on a "moneyed basis" and to allow domination of the enterprise by the wealthy.

Concern lest those of "long missionary experience and true missionary ardor" be overruled by an ill-informed and inexperienced majority led to a third argument set forth in the report. Surprisingly enough, the new basis of membership was not only more democratic but also fostered all the values of aristocracy. The life membership principle provides "a class of members, who from their fixed position and tenure of a permanent influence, will have an acquaintance and an experience in the management of missions that could not be secured under the older system." Since they are removed from the pressures implicit in the principle of representation and need give no thought to the point of view of a constituency in order to be returned as delegates for another year, they can give mature and impartial consideration to all questions. Thus, the acrimony and strife of party debate will be eliminated.

A fourth argument set forth in the report is closely related to the third: the new set-up is much more efficient. "Our past missionary history," said the report, "shows the inconvenient and embarrassing character of the old platform." Since "the old platform" had provided a means—in the form of delegates—by which the diverse sentiments of the people in the churches might find expression, the meetings of the Convention became occasions for controversy. The "paramount object of evangelizing the nations for Christ" was often forgotten, and other topics were debated in the deliberative assemblies. This had led to a waning of missionary zeal. The only efficient method for missionary operations, therefore, was to divorce them from the churches entirely and to carry them on by voluntary societies which make their appeal only to the individual conscience. This has been the experience even of "those religious communions of our own day who have held most tenaciously the doctrine that we repudiate, of a great visible and earthly church, and that this church is the only competent missionary organization." They have not been able to succeed in making their "ecclesiastical communion" "an efficient missionary organization." Baptists have much to learn in this respect, asserted the report, from Roman Catholics. "The most efficient missionary institution of Rome herself, perfect as is her ecclesiastical machinery, are not . . . ecclesiastical organizations but voluntary societies—the Lyons Society in France and the Leopold Foundation in Austria—appealing each of them to individual contributors and receiving each what it may be able to solicit, not what it can assess and levy."

Having demonstrated that the new system had all the values of both democracy and aristocracy, that it could be defended from either side of the money question, and that it commended itself in terms of its efficiency of operation; the report proceeded to justify the change by an appeal to historic Baptist principles. Authors of the report had admitted that the shift from annual representation to life membership was new, that it was an innovation that should at least be given a fair trial, and that opposition to it was largely motivated by a desire to cling to old ways of doing things. But now it was to be argued that actually the old was the new, that the innovation was no innovation at all but merely the traditional Baptist pattern and practice.

Baptists have always believed, it was said, that "the church of the Scriptures, where it is a visible church, is a single local congregation of faithful men," and they have "contended that the single Christian congregation has no earthly ecclesiastical organization above it." Baptists, of course, "have recognized the right, the privilege, and the duty of cooperation among these several churches," but they "have protested loudly and sternly, and contended even to the death, against the right of any council or association, meeting in the name of the churches, to lord it over their discipline or doctrine." The report then asked the question: "What is our denominational mode of obtaining cooperation as churches?" To which it gave this answer:

> We express union and sympathy, as independent churches, by *delegates* and by *epistles*. The epistle is the written delegate; the delegate is the oral epistle. . . . The word for delegates which our fathers delighted to employ was the scriptural term "the messengers of the churches."

What this meant, if it meant anything at all, was that there is no method of cooperation among the churches, only a means of communication.

In spite of the fact that "our fathers" ever since the founding of the Philadelphia Association in 1707 had been accustomed to using "delegate" and "representative" as synonymous and interchangeable terms, the report asserted that they are not equivalent terms.

> The delegate is not a representative. . . . A representative *presents* in some remote spot, as if in person there, the individual or the body sending him; and his presence binds on the party sending him all the legitimate acts of the conference to which they thus sent him.

Baptists must be careful not to "confound our *voluntary* organizations with our *ecclesiastical*" by "the dangerous principle of church *representation.*" For representation includes *legislation,* and legislation, "in all fairness," includes or ought to include *taxation.* Any society based upon representation, "claiming the right to represent and embody law for the churches," should be able to "raise assessors to fix on our wealthier churches and on our church members the quota due from their affluence, but denied by their covetousness, to the work of evangelization."

This curious semantic argument served only to confuse the issue. Representatives are always sent for definite purposes. No one was suggesting that delegates from Baptist churches should serve as "assessors" to levy "taxes." The question was whether or not the churches were to have any voice in determining how the common funds to which they had contributed would be used. Should a mission be established in Assam or Liberia? Should the missionaries itinerate or should they occupy fixed stations? Should agents be employed to solicit funds? Decisions like these were not the internal concerns of any church; they were the common concern of all the churches, at least of those churches which contributed to the mission funds. The real issue was whether these questions should be decided by men who, having been given life tenure, were in no way responsible to those who gave the money, or decided by men who were sent as delegates for this purpose from the contributing churches. Actually, of course, representatives of Baptist churches had always been accustomed to meet in joint deliberation to discuss and to decide the course to be pursued in matters of common concern.

The final appeal of the report was to Scripture. It seemed clear, to the authors of the report, that there could be no objection to purely "voluntary organizations" for "certain administrative purposes," provided they were completely divorced from the churches and had no ecclesiastical basis. Such a divorce, to be sure, made it possible for non-Baptists and even non-Christians to become life members of the Missionary Union by contributing one hundred dollars to its funds. If objections were to be raised at this point, one should turn to the Bible and ask: "How were missions conducted of old ? Have ours a scriptural pattern? Did the first Christians repudiate all aid from the world?" When these questions are asked, the answer becomes clear. The apostle Paul received help from the heathen in his travels, and Christ himself, "the only infallible and perfect missionary the world ever saw or ever shall see, received, if not money, yet money's worth in his missionary travels, from every host at whose table he sat or under whose roof or within whose fishing bark he was received." Simon the leper, Zacchaeus the publican, "the woman whose alabaster box anointed him for burial; all were missionary contributors, and Christ received their offerings to forward his missionary career." Thus there is no question that "the Christian missionary may receive aid for his missionary work from others than acknowledged Christians."

At this point, there follows one of the most curious digressions in the report. Christ may have received aid from unbelievers, but he did not give them a vote to determine where and when and what he should preach, and the report attempts to forestall this objection.

> The world, it would seem, may share in the work. But should they control it? Certainly not. The churches should govern it. But how so? Are missionary organizations to be made, formally and authoritatively, a part of our church economy? Have we a scriptural warrant for that? The missions of the Christian church, in their earliest and most missionary era, do not seem to have been sustained by a great ecclesiastical fund, authoritatively levied, and which ecclesiastical rulers were formally to dispense. It seems to have been then, as now, left very much to the individual conscience.

The remarkable feature of this passage is that the rhetorical question is never answered. The world should not control the mission fund; the churches should govern it. But the "how" remained unanswered.

The authors of the report went on to complete their *tour de force* by emphasizing that it is our duty to avoid all "human policy" and to hold fast to "the simpler and wiser safeguards of Christ's own providing."

> The helm is not given to our weak and mortal hands. The Pilot who points the prow and watches the heavens to guide our missionary way is older than the stars and [older] than the keel of the missionary church he guides; for he is the Ancient of Days, and his goings forth have been from everlasting. Christ, by his Spirit working in his people, is the great executive agency of the missionary work. Missionary societies are but a portion of the voluntary and fiscal arrangements of the crew amongst themselves, but which neither control the course of the voyage nor construct the chart.

Christ's constitution is "the scriptural, local, and independent church." If the day should ever come when we "should make the membership of our missionary societies strictly and fully representative of the churches, sitting as their legislators and their assessors, enacting the statute and levying the contingent of taxation," it would be "a day of gloom for the churches at home and for our missionary colonies abroad." It would mean that "the first and decisive step" had been taken "in the way to Rome." Only time and "Satan's vigilant activity" would be needed "to bring in all the rest—the crosier, the canon, the tiara, and the Pontiff—infallibility and despotism and Antichrist."

The Committee of Nine closed its report with the suggestion that an inquiry be made among those who were described as the "honest friends of missions in the churches" to determine their opinion on the question of altering the constitution. These "true and warm friends of missions" were, of course, the life members of the Union. It should not have been necessary to poll them on the report for they were supposed to have been present at the annual meeting. They could scarcely be said to represent a cross section of the denomination, nor as life members who had already paid their one hundred dollars could they be regarded as an entirely unprejudiced jury. And when it is recalled that the whole weight and prestige of the officers of the Union were cast on one side of the question and that the report of the Committee of Nine was sent to the members with the letter of inquiry, the result would seem to have been a foregone conclusion.

In view of all these circumstances, it is astonishing to discover that when the results of the poll were announced at the next annual meeting (1849), the vote was very close. It was only 419 to 412 against altering the constitution. The closeness of the vote, with the early returns known to the headquarters in Boston, would suggest that there had been some heavy campaigning during the last month or two in order to secure even that narrow margin. A majority of life members in all states except Maine, Massachusetts, Rhode Island, Pennsylvania, and New Jersey were in favor of adding annual members from the churches. It was only a heavy negative vote in Massachusetts and especially in Wayland's bailiwick of Rhode Island that shifted the final vote to slight majority against any change. The committee which had been appointed to examine the returns compiled by the corresponding secretary of the Home Department reported that, since "the Union can make no alteration in the constitution except by a vote of two-thirds of the members present at an annual meeting and only upon the recommendation of the Board of Managers," it was their belief that any further discussion of the subject should be indefinitely postponed.

VIII

Stripped of its pious verbiage, the scheme that resulted in forming the American Baptist Foreign Missionary Union had a simple objective— to bypass the long discussions and sometimes "angry altercations" involved in the democratic process, and to place the missionary enterprise firmly in the control of those who had "long missionary experience and true missionary ardor." Francis Wayland was quite explicit at this point. By excluding "all semblance of representation," every member

> speaks for himself, and for himself alone. He can throw the blame of his actions on no constituents, but must stand up and answer to the public for himself. This has been a great advantage, and has tended to save us from many a useless, angry, and partisan discussion. The membership is also much more permanent, and so little time is not occupied by brethren who, for the first time, have attended a general missionary meeting and are wholly ignorant of the subject of missions.[18]

Actually, the life members, who were at the annual meetings to speak only for themselves and not for the churches, had little to discuss. Their function, as Wayland pointed out, was to elect members of the Board, which would elect the Executive Committee that had "the special management of the concerns of missions." To be sure, the life members did listen to some reports, but their only other business was to designate the next place of meeting, to appoint someone to preach the annual sermon, and to adopt a resolution tendering thanks "to the railroad and steamboat companies which, with great liberality, have conveyed the members over their different routes at reduced fare."

Ultimately, like the idea of having each denominational concern promoted by a separate society proceeding independently with its own agents to solicit funds, the whole concept of leaving the direction of missionary affairs in the hands of a denomination-al elite broke down. Not even the life members were content to be treated as puppets, and the churches—controlling the purse strings—demanded a voice in making the decisions. Life member-ship was abolished entirely in favor of direct representation by delegates from the churches.

In the meantime, however, Francis Wayland had been busy publicizing and popularizing his views with what can only be described as the skill of a Madison Avenue technician. He felt no hesitancy in playing upon fears and appealing to prejudices then widely current in America in order to win support for his schemes to consolidate control in the hands of the few. He played tricks with words. He twisted arguments. He utilized digressions to cloud and obscure the issue. Every success of his intrigues he attributed to "the sturdy common sense of the masses of our Brethren." He described himself as "an old-fashioned Baptist," but he was anything but that. He spoke of that unhappy interval when the Triennial Convention had experimented with the principle of representation, when he well knew that this had been the traditional practice of Baptists in associational life. He described the Triennial Convention as "the only representative organization ever attempted among us," when he knew that this was not true. In setting forth his novel ideas, he would assert that "these have always been favorite ideas with our Baptist churches" and that this was what "Baptists have ever believed." Those who differed from him, he accused of violating "the precepts of Jesus."

Wayland set forth his views on a variety of topics in a series of articles in the *Examiner,* which were collected and published in 1857 under the title *Notes on the Principles and Practices of Baptist Churches.* The book, homely in style and pithy in expression, met a real need for a manual for Baptist churches. Therefore, it had an astonishing sale and went through at least five editions. The unfortunate consequence of this was that shibboleths invented for the campaigns of 1826 and 1846, which were set forth and defended in two of the essays in this book, by this means as much as any other, deeply penetrated the consciousness of Baptists everywhere.

Thus, the machinations of a small group of men have left us with a two-fold legacy—one organizational, and the other ideological. The organizational disorder among Baptists in the North is most apparent at the national level where it has thus far defied all attempts to make the national structure an efficient and responsible instrument of the churches. A more serious consequence has been the bypassing of the local Association, which is the most important unit in the whole denominational structure. All significant functions of the Associations have been taken away, and they have been left to eke out a bootless existence. Equally serious has been the abandonment of the proposal to extend the association principle through the state conventions to the national convention. This has meant, on the one hand, that most of the churches have been effectively disfranchised; on the other hand, it has meant that the national convention has been too large to be an effective deliberative body.

But it is the ideological legacy that has been the heaviest burden. Although Wayland's schemes proved unworkable and were discarded, Baptists have suffered a persistently guilty conscience with regard to their present denominational practices. Wayland's reinterpretation of Baptist history lives on to haunt us and to frustrate earnest endeavors to make some sense of our denominational structure. The heritage of disorganization is most complete in the North, but it is in the South that Wayland's ideas made their deepest inroads. In the South, the pre-1826 structure remains largely unchanged (although still incomplete in terms of the associational principle) but it is undergirded by a theory of communication, not of cooperation.

NOTES

[1] *American Baptist Magazine*, III, 435.
[2] *Ibid.*, IV, 376.
[3] *Ibid.*, VI, 118.
[4] *Ibid.*
[5] *New York Baptist Register*, I, 25.
[6] *Ibid.*, II, 65.
[7] *Ibid.*, 175.
[8] *Ibid.*, I, 306.
[9] *Ibid.*, II, 163.
[10] *American Baptist Magazine*, IV, 455.
[11] *Ibid.*, V, iv.

[12] Francis and H. L. Wayland, *A Memoir of Francis Wayland*, I, 180.

[13] *Ibid.*, 195. James O. Murray, *Francis Wayland*, 43.

[14] *American Baptist Magazine*, IV, 324-328.

[15] *Ibid.*, VI, 114–119.

[16] *Ibid.*, 209.

[17] *Thirty-fourth Annual Report of the American Baptist Missionary Union* (1848), 111-128

[18] *Notes on the Principles and Practices of Baptist Churches*, 187-188.

6
Divergent Careers of Northern and Southern Baptists

The dramatic contrast between the growth of the Southern Baptist Convention and the American Baptist Convention [Churches] has intrigued many people and has been the subject of much speculation. Why is it that Southern Baptists have multiplied in number, while American Baptists have lagged in growth? Answers to this question usually have been sought in simple polarities which are assumed to have been distinctive of the two conventions; for example, a zeal for souls on the one side versus humanitarian concerns on the other, an otherworldly understanding of the Christian faith versus a this-worldly understanding of the Christian faith, a strong emphasis upon Baptist distinctives versus a temporizing ecumenical spirit, and a highly structured denominational program versus locally adapted denominational activities. While such polarities may have existed to a greater or lesser degree and may have contributed to the strength or weakness of the two conventions, they do not by themselves constitute an adequate explanation of differing rates of growth. They do not take fully into account the separate careers of the two conventions, careers which in some respects have been so diverse that parallels and polarities are not always relevant. Each convention must be understood within its own context and upon its own terms. Furthermore, the establishment of simple polarities does not take into account the fact that rates of growth have not been constant in either convention.

Accurate statistics, of course, are difficult to secure and difficult to assess. Nonetheless, on the basis of statistics assembled and explained in appended tables, it seems clear that marked Southern Baptist growth occurred, first, in the period from 1850 to 1870; second, in the period from 1900 to 1912; and, third, in the period from 1920 to 1960. American Baptists, on the other hand, maintained a steady rate of growth until the end of World War I, after which they were barely able to maintain their total number of adherents. These periods have been identified for the most part by decades, and therefore they are not always precise for any single year. On July 16, 1921, *The Baptist*, for example, noted with ill-concealed pleasure that in 1920, the year which is given as delimiting the beginning of a period of marked Southern Baptist growth and of American Baptist stagnation, American Baptists had one baptism for every twelve members whereas Southern Baptists had only one baptism for every seventeen members. Still, in spite of occasional spurts and declines which ran counter to the general trend, the periodization is accurate enough to be suggestive and illuminating.

I

A surprising feature of the Southern Baptist pattern of growth is the surge in numbers which took place between 1850 and 1870. Southern and American Baptists were roughly equal in size in 1850, if some allowance is made for the numbers of blacks who were counted in the Southern Baptist total. American Baptists exhibited a healthy growth, increasing by 66 percent during the two decades from 1850 to 1870. Using an 1850 base figure for Southern Baptists, which includes many blacks not represented in the 1870 totals, Southern Baptists—even with this inflated base— posted an astonishing increase of 102 percent during the two decades. Both groups undoubtedly profited from the quiet revival which was so pervasive in the years immediately preceding the Civil War. The additional Southern Baptist growth may be attributed in part to a continuing revival in Confederate army camps where the spirit of the troops was bolstered by informal prayer meetings and preaching services, and in part to a supposition that in defeat people of the South found extra solace in the promises of the gospel.

Almost equally surprising as the increase which marked the decades bracketing the Civil War is the steady growth of Southern Baptists in the decades from 1870 to 1900, a rate of growth which closely paralleled that of American Baptists. This is surprising, for the greater portion of this period usually has been portrayed as a period of near collapse among Southern Baptists. Just as enthusiastic Methodist historians have often depicted English religious life during the initial decades of the eighteenth century in unduly gloomy terms in order to throw into sharp relief the achievements of John Wesley, so one suspects that Southern Baptists in similar fashion have often sought to justify and magnify the shift in direction represented by Isaac Taylor Tichenor by stressing the near bankruptcy of Southern Baptists prior to the time when he and his supporters began to take things in hand.

II

While nineteenth-century statistics are helpful in assessing Southern Baptist vigor and vitality, it is the multiplying number of Southern Baptists in the twentieth century which requires careful analysis. Several factors undoubtedly contributed to Southern Baptist growth, such as evangelistic zeal, relative isolation from the corrosive effects of "modernity," a homogeneous population, carefully devised "growth techniques," and a constituency with a relatively high birthrate. But perhaps the most important factor was the role of the Southern Baptist Convention as the only available vehicle for the institutional expression of Southern regional sentiment. Politically the South was divided into several states. Economically the post-Civil War commercial and industrial ventures of the South were tied to northern financial centers. The Southern Presbyterian Church in the United States, the Methodist Episcopal Church, South, and the Southern Baptist Convention were the only institutional links which bound the South together. Of these three groups, only the Methodists and Baptists had a broad enough constituency and a sufficiently popular appeal to provide a mass base for the expression of sectional feeling.

When the *Charleston Mercury* commented in 1845 that the division of the Methodists and Baptists meant that henceforth "in the two most numerous denominations of the country" there would be "a northern and a southern religion," it was only partially correct.[1] The tendency of the postwar years in the churches was toward reconciliation and reunion. Episcopalians, Disciples, Lutherans, and Roman Catholics quickly restored the bonds which had been broken by civil strife. Presbyterians, Methodists, and Baptists faced a more difficult problem, for their division had antedated the conflict and their separation had become more institutionalized and thus more deeply rooted. Nevertheless, they also tended to look forward to a restoration of the ties which had been severed. Only gradually did a growing nostalgia begin to idealize and romanticize the antebellum years and nurture the growing conviction that Southerners were "a different people" set apart from the rest of the nation.

As early as 1880, the *New Orleans Christian Advocate* declared the "civilization" of the South and "the customs and character of the people" were quite different from those of the North.

> One broad distinction is that the Southerner, as a matter of honor and principle, minds his own business, while the inborn nature of the North is to meddle. The South is tolerant, courteous, and refined in its contact with people in the ordinary associations of life. The North has a prying, inquisitive disposition, and is bent on bringing every one to its way of thinking and doing.[2]

There were also, the *Advocate* asserted, differences in religion.

> There is a south side to churches and religion, not so much in regard to their creeds . . . as in the type of piety that prevails. Methodists and Presbyterians in the South profess the same faith as Methodists and Presbyterians in the North, and yet they are not the same people. The political meddling of the northern churches is, of course, one difference. . . . There is a secularity about them, and a style that brings them into near fellowship with worldly enterprises and organizations. They *run* things up there—churches as well as factories and railroads. The style of their preaching is in contrast with ours, and is largely of the politico-sensational order. The North has been over-run with evangelists whose methods and teachings have in many instances done harm. People raised in these churches and imbued with their spirit, if converted, are apt to be essentially defective in the higher traits of Christian character. With many excellent people and exemplary Christians among them, and with much that is good and worthy of imitation in their church work, there is a spirit and practice, and a type or religion, that we should regret to see in our southern churches.[3]

Fortunately or unfortunately, the *New Orleans Christian Advocate* did not represent the center of power in southern Methodism. In 1874 southern Methodist leadership had begun to prepare the way for an eventual rapprochement with the northern church. While this policy evoked dissent and even dismay in some quarters, leaders who insisted that "there is but *one* Episcopal Methodism in the United States" remained firmly in control of southern Methodism's centralized system of polity.[4] Restrained by this official stance, southern Methodists were inhibited from becoming fully effective bearers and custodians of regional sentiment.

III

A different situation prevailed among Southern Baptists. Until the last decade of the century it was not clear in which direction Southern Baptists would move—toward closer ties with Baptists of the North or toward continued separation and independence. Even prior to the Civil War there had been a somewhat marked difference between Baptists in the North and in the South. Although there was no uniformity in either section, Baptists in the North tended to be middle class, tended to think in terms of an educated ministry, and expanded westward by the rise of missionaries.[5] Baptists in the South, on the other hand, tended to be of lower social and economic status, exhibited much less interest in an educated ministry, and expanded westward by means of farmer preachers.[6] One is tempted to suggest that Baptists in the South had been assimilated to Separatist Baptist emphases, while Baptists in the North adhered to an older Regular Baptist ethos.[7] But this idea would miss the mark. The difference was more cultural than religious. Actually, Baptists in New England were largely Separates in background, and Separates in the South were the product of the evangelistic activity of New England Separates. As the result of this activity the back country of the South became a great bastion of Baptist strength. What occurred is that Baptists of the two sections were quickly assimilated into the prevailing culture of the regions which constituted the base of their support. Thus there was something of a cleavage among Baptists that was not based on the slavery issue, even before 1845.

After the Civil War the same tendency toward reconciliation was present among Baptists as among members of other denominations. The American Baptist Home Mission Society had warm friends and received generous support in the South. The American Baptist Publication Society solicited contributions at meetings of Southern Baptist state conventions and associations, maintained "book rooms" in Atlanta and Dallas, and supplied the publication needs of Southern Baptist churches. Baptist Congresses, which began to be held in 1882, drew representatives from North and South alike. The Baptist Young People's Union was organized in 1891 on a national basis. In 1879, when I. T. Tichenor proposed a resolution at the Southern Baptist Convention advocating cordial cooperation between Baptists of the North and South, John A. Broadus and W. H. Whitsitt understood the overture to be a step toward dissolving the line of division. Tichenor's intention, however, was exactly the reverse. He was seeking to strengthen the Southern Baptist Convention by insisting upon a clear-cut allocation of territory.

The growing sectional feeling in the South carried the day in the Southern Baptist Convention. R. B. Spain notes the resurgence of sectional feeling in the 1890s.[8] Perhaps this feeling was intensified among Southern Baptists by the tactlessness and seeming arrogance of the American Baptist Home Mission Society ("North America for Christ" was its slogan). Certainly sectional feeling was allowed full play in a polity designed to be responsive to the appeals of popular leaders rather than to the more sober counsels of elder statesmen. In any event, under the leadership of Tichenor, who became secretary of the Southern Baptist Home Mission Board in 1882, the die was cast. In 1894 the respective Home Mission agencies agreed to an allocation of territory and by roughly 1900 the separation was complete, a separation that was formalized by the organization of the Northern (American) Baptist Convention in 1907.[9]

As one reads Southern Baptist literature, one immediately becomes aware of a strong "Southern" self-consciousness, of a constant emphasis upon "southwide" needs and "southwide" causes, of an outlook which Rufus B. Spain has described as "intensely Southern,"[10] and of attitudes which reflect the prevailing convictions and mores of the South. The South is described in promotional literature as though it is a national entity in itself. In the words of J. B. Lawrence, "The Southland is a vast empire of untold wealth and religious possibilities. In richness there is no country like it in the world."[11] Small wonder that the Southern Baptist Convention, at a time of growing southern regional self-consciousness, began to play the role of the established national churches of eastern and southern Europe.

IV

The Southern Baptist Convention, as the major regional denomination in an area dominated by a regional mystique, profited greatly from its almost complete identification with "the Southern way of life." As a thoroughly "popular" denomination, it gained additional recruits from within its carefully circumscribed ambit. Then, as Southerners moved westward and as mixed areas such as Missouri succumbed more fully to the southern mystique, the Mason-Dixon line was extended in the minds of Southern Baptists so that new territory might be included within the bounds of the Southland. American Baptists in Oklahoma and New Mexico were bluntly informed that they should work "their own territory." Baptists in southern Illinois had toppled into Southern Baptist ranks in 1907, ostensibly because the isolation of Southern Baptists had preserved their orthodoxy in contrast to the heterodoxy seeping into American Baptist life from the University of Chicago. Presumably the traditional ties of the area with the South were at least equally important. Cairo, the capital of the Illinois Egypt, it should be remembered, was located about halfway between St. Louis and the Mississippi border.

A totally new situation arose during and following World War II when Southerners found themselves uprooted from their homeland and relocated in army camps and factories in distant parts of the United States. Never before was the power of sectional identification more dramatically demonstrated. Many Southern Baptist displaced persons were not content to join American Baptist churches, no matter how orthodox the latter might be. What was of importance was the Southern Baptist name and the Southern Baptist "Program." After some anguish, the Southern Baptist Home Mission Board discovered that the Great Commission was not subject to territorial delimitation, and that the former agreement to abide by a territorial allocation had been a mistake. Finally, even after the Southern Baptist Convention had been operating on a national basis for a decade and a half, no proposal was more firmly resisted than the suggestion that "Southern" be dropped from the name of the Convention. This regional identification remained important both to its identity and to its appeal.

V

Baptists in the North had a somewhat different history. In 1830 approximately one-third of all Baptists in the United States were to be found in New England and New York. This was the great bastion of Baptist strength in the North. C. C. Goen has noted that at the outset Baptists in Connecticut represented a fair cross section of the population.[12] In several places in New Hampshire the Baptist church was the town church, although these churches tended to develop qualms about having the pastor's salary paid out of town rates. With the passage of years and the movement of population westward, Baptists of Yankee origin tended to rise in social status. Whitney R. Cross, in a careful study of "the burned-over district," reported that Congregationalists who had turned Presbyterian and Baptists were the two upper-class denominations in central and western New York in contrast to the lower-class denominations—Methodists, Universalists, Free-Will Baptists, and Christians.[13] Baptists were somewhat more numerous than Presbyterians, while the Presbyterians had an advantage in wealth and education. "Upper-class" is a relative term, and in central and western New York prior to 1850 it referred to the more prosperous farmers and small town merchants. To some extent the term referred to cultural and social aspiration, an aspiration that found partial fulfillment among Baptists in a preoccupation with establishing academies throughout the state. As the New England stream of migration moved through New York into the Middle West, Baptists continued to maintain, broadly speaking, a middle-class status and to embrace persons of wealth within their ranks. The preoccupation with education culminated in the 1890s with the founding of the University of Chicago.

Until World War I, Baptists remained a leading denomination across the northern tier of states. In a reasonable proportion of localities, the Baptist church possessed the tallest steeple, the symbol of the economic status of the congregation. In Des Moines, Iowa, the Baptist church had been the first to be built in the fashionable residential area on the hill. In Chicago, as elsewhere, the names of leading citizens graced the membership rolls. While not an upper-class denomination in the modern sense of the world, still Baptists had social status and social prestige. Nor did these Northern Baptists lag perceptibly in numerical growth. Each decade after 1870 the gain in membership averaged 25 percent, an increase that matched a population growth swollen by immigrants of Roman Catholic, Eastern Orthodox, and Jewish background. Also during the period from 1870 to 1890, the Northern Baptist rate of growth was approximately the same as that of Southern Baptists.

After World War I, Northern Baptist growth slowed to a crawl and then came to a full stop. Northern Baptists were beset by the same problems of immigration, urbanization, industrialization, population mobility, technological change, and a shifting intellectual climate that troubled the life of other churches in the North. But Northern Baptists had a further problem of their own.

VI

Northern Baptists were more deeply divided, distracted, and immobilized by the Fundamentalist controversy than any other denomination. Among Baptists, each minister's pulpit is his throne. He is subject to no ecclesiastical control if he can carry his congregation with him. With this freedom and denied such sectional isolation and insulation as was enjoyed by Southern Baptists, Northern Baptists closely paralleled Congregationalists in providing an undue proportion of the leadership which responded in positive fashion to new biblical and scientific studies. By the same token, the opposition which this evoked could not be quelled by any ecclesiastical decree. No firm decision on a compromise settlement to end the controversy could be made. Throughout the twenties, thirties, and forties, the issue had to be faced at each annual convention as well as to be fought out in local areas and congregations.

Not only did the controversy immobilize the denomination, but also the bitterness and invective with which it was carried on gave Baptists throughout the North a bad public image. The denomination began to leak at both ends and in the middle. Organized Fundamentalist defections took place in the 1920s, in the 1930s, and again in the 1940s. Furthermore, irenically inclined conservatives, as well as irenically inclined liberals, often opted out and joined some other church where they could raise their families in a more peaceful and, as they believed, in a more Christian atmosphere. Moreover, as a result of the controversy, the Baptist image had small appeal to potential recruits. In a given church, many potential members, before they could be enticed into membership, first had to be persuaded that this specific church was not like other Baptist churches.

The Fundamentalist controversy was the major factor that accounts for the marked reversal in Northern Baptist fortunes in the twentieth century—a controversy that distracted and immobilized the denomination and gave it an unattractive public image. A loose, lax, and easy liberalism may ultimately have sapped Baptist vitality, but in a religious climate which minimized theological and denominational differences, it scarcely accounts for the precipitate shift in fortune. A striking feature of the Northern Baptist plight was the reversal of the usual upward progression in social status of American denominations, a progression from the wrong side of the tracks to the right side of the tracks. During the past half century, Northern, now American, Baptists have provided an illustration of a denomination steadily declining in social status. While Southern Baptists also have a problem of leakage at the top, it is probable that in its own heartland the Southern Baptist Convention now has much greater social status and social prestige than the American Baptist Convention [Churches] has in any part of its constituency. There also are indications that the educational level of the two constituencies is not greatly dissimilar.

VII

Several questions face Southern Baptists as they look to the future. Will they be able, or even wish, to maintain a regional identity that capitalizes upon sectional feelings? Even if they do wish to and are able to do so, will a regional identity still have as strong an appeal as heretofore? Furthermore, with the South having emerged from its isolation, will Southern Baptists be able to maintain sufficient cohesiveness to avoid the strife which fragmented, immobilized, and discredited American Baptists? Population mobility often obscures what amounts to an actual drop in membership. When Northern Baptists began reporting nonresident members in 1932, it was an effort to give insiders a more realistic appraisal of the true strength of the Convention. The fact that nonresidents were carried on the membership rolls also was an indication of a growing laxity in membership standards. When Southern Baptists began to report nonresident members in 1960, it also was a reflection that a central covenant obligation was being widely ignored, and it also indicated that perhaps as much as a quarter of the reported number of Southern Baptists was little more than a paper membership. Southern Baptist decline may already have begun. If so, can the decline be checked? Will a plateau period ensue with the possibilities of renewed growth or drastic decline?

COMPARATIVE STATISTICS

Any reliable church statistics are difficult enough to secure. Comparative statistics between the Southern and American Baptist Conventions are doubly difficult to ascertain. This is partly because reports were not always complete, and partly because the two groups sometimes claimed overlapping membership. For this reason, in the following tables, membership figures were omitted for both groups from Missouri, Oklahoma, and District of Columbia prior to 1920. Missouri, of course, was the only state during these years that would have made any significant difference. A further complication is that figures for Southern Baptists intermittently included Baptists. Primitive Baptists, Landmarkists, and Gospel Missioners. Where this has occurred, an attempt has been made to subtract these totals so that an accurate comparison can be made.

Nineteenth-century comparison.[14]

Southern Baptist Convention	American Baptist Convention
1850 343,000 (SBC 10% larger, but identification of black members incomplete[15])	312,000
1870 693,047—102% increase (SBC 34% larger)	517,673—66% increase
1880 850,427—22½% increase (SBC 37% larger)	617,766—22% increase
1890 1,141,282—34¼% increase (SBC 38½% larger)	823,016—33% increase
1900 1,482,274—30% increase (SBC 47% larger)	1,008,252—22½% increase

Early twentieth-century comparison.[16]

Southern Baptist Convention	Northern Baptist Convention
1912 2,200,948—48½% increase from 1900 (SBC 81% larger)	1,214,997—20½% increase from 1900.
1918 2,425,734—10.2% increase (SBC 83½% larger)	1,321,750—8.8% increase
1920 2,492,236—2.7% increase (SBC 98% larger)	1,253,878—5% *decrease*

Post-World War I comparison[17]

Southern Baptist Convention	American Baptist Convention
1920 2,781,642	1,253,878
1925 3,520,513—27% increase	1,382,342—10¼% increase
1930 3,850,278—9½% increase	1,438,739—4% increase
1935 4,389,417—14% increase	1,458,811—1½% increase (226,230 nonresident)[18]
1940 5,104,327—16% increase	1,561,289—7% increase (249,094 nonresident)
1945 5,865,544—13% increase	1,592,349—2% increase (401,782 nonresident)
1950 7,079,889—20½% increase	1,554,304—2½% *decrease* (319,162 nonresident)

1955 8,474,741—18% increase   1,528,210—1½% *decrease*
                                       (296,567 nonresident)
1960 9,731,591—15% increase   1,521,052—½% *decrease*
      (2,607,047 nonresident)   (246,113 nonresident)
1965 10,772,712—10½% in-   1,557,633—2% increase [19]
      crease   (462,020 nonresident)
      (2,894,492 nonresident)

NOTES

[1] W. B. Posey, *The Baptist Church in the Lower Mississippi Valley, 1776-1845* (Lexington: University of Kentucky Press, 1957), p. 154.

[2] W. S. Hudson, *Religion in America* (New York: Charles Scribner's Sons, 1965), p. 218.

[3] *Ibid.*

[4] E. S. Bucke, ed., *The History of Methodism* (New York: Abingdon Press, 1964), vol. 3, p. 409.

[5] W. R. Cross, *The Burned-Over District: The Social and Intellectual History of Enthusiastic Religion in Western New York, 1800-1850* (Ithaca: Cornell University Press, 1950), pp. 8, 18, 46, 101, 102.

[6] From Louis B. Wright, *Culture on the Moving Frontier* (Bloomington: Indiana University Press, 1955), pp. 51-52.

[7] W. L. Lumpkin, *Baptist Foundations in the South: Tracing Through the Influence of the Great Awakening* (Nashville: The Broadman Press, 1961).

[8] Rufus B. Spain, *At Ease in Zion: Social History of the Southern Baptists, 1865-1900* (Nashville: Vanderbilt University Press, 1967), pp. 28-29.

[9] See Donnell R. Harris, "The Gradual Separation of Southern and Northern Baptists, 1845-1907," *Foundations*, vol. 7, no. 2 (April-June, 1964), pp. 130-144.

[10] Spain, *op. cit.*, p. 210.

[11] J. B. Lawrence, *Home Missions in the New World* (Atlanta: Home Mission Board of the Southern Baptist Convention, 1943), p. 83.

[12] C. C. Goen, *Revivalism and Separatism in New England, 1740-1800* (New Haven: Yale University Press, 1962), p. 191.

[13] Cross, *op. cit.*, p. 46.

[14] Source: *American Baptist Register* for 1852 and the *Northern Baptist Yearbook* for 1872, 1882, 1892, and 1902. The totals represent association reports for the preceding year which, in turn, represent church reports for the prior year. Missouri, Oklahoma, and District of Columbia figures were deleted throughout. What is needed is a study of statistics church by church in association reports. Only in this way can random variation be detected. Also there was an error in simple addition of 50,000 members in the statistics for Mississippi in the 1902 *Yearbook*. This error was then reproduced in totals for the South and for the United States as a whole.

[15] After the Civil War, black churches and black associations were usually identified and in the latter decades were given separate totals. In 1850 some churches and some associations reported the number of black members, and the reported black membership has been subtracted from the Southern Baptist total. Still, 58 percent of the associations in Alabama, Georgia, Kentucky, Louisiana, Mississippi, North Carolina, South Carolina, and Georgia did not report how many blacks were included in their membership totals. Furthermore, in those associations which did give black membership figures, there were many churches which did not provide this information. Even a minimum estimate of unreported blacks would cancel the 10 percent margin in number of members of the Southern Baptist Convention over the Northern Baptist constituency in 1850. If allowance were made for this in establishing a more accurate 1850 base figure for Southern Baptists, the increase in

1870 would jump from the astonishing 102 percent to an even more remarkable 120 percent.

[16] Source: The *Annuals* of the two conventions. The figures are taken from the *Annuals* of the succeeding year, where they represent totals for the preceding year and possibly church reports for the year prior to the year assigned. The year 1912 was selected because of a certain degree of confusion. By 1912 the situation between the two conventions had been stabilized. Landmarkists ceased to cooperate with Southern Baptists beginning in 1902, and southern Illinois associations defected to the Southern Baptist Convention in 1910. Oklahoma and Missouri remained in contention. The Northern Baptist Convention ceased reporting Oklahoma figures in 1915 and Missouri figures in 1919. For comparative purposes, Oklahoma and Missouri figures have been subtracted from the totals of both conventions. Also the estimates of nonreported members, the membership of black churches were identified, and the membership of mission churches abroad have been subtracted from the Southern Baptist totals. Finally, the 136,420 members of Landmarkist and Gospel Mission associations have been subtracted from the 1920 Southern Baptist total. Then to make the earlier figures roughly comparable, 130,000 has been subtracted from the totals for 1912 and 1918. Southern Baptist Annuals ceased including these associations in 1926, almost 25 years after any nominal cooperation had ended. The 1918 figure is included to indicate that the Southern Baptist Convention temporarily tightened its statistical reporting in 1920.

[17] Source: All figures are from the convention *Annuals* of the succeeding year. Where identified, non-Southern Baptist figures have been subtracted from the Southern Baptist totals for 1920 and 1925. The practice of including these figures ceased in 1926. The membership figures for Missouri and Oklahoma, deleted from the 1920 Southern Baptist total in the preceding "Early Twentieth Century Comparison," have been restored here in the "Post-World War I Comparison," for the affiliation of Missouri and Oklahoma was no longer in contention.

[18] American Baptists began to identify nonresident members in 1932. The effort to do so met with varying success, with the result that the nonresident (sometimes identified as inactive) portion of the total was never completely identified.

[19] This American Baptist gain in 1965 of 36,581 was more than canceled by a 215,807 gain in the nonresident portion of the total membership. Southern Baptist reports of nonresident members included in the totals in 1960 and 1965 make it clear that similar questions concerning Southern Baptist membership figures had been arising. In both conventions, the nonresident figures reflect population mobility and a growing laxity of membership standards.

7
Shifting Patterns of Church Order, 1900-1935

In 1900 American Baptists possessed as distin-
guished a galaxy of theologians as any denomination in the United
States. At Newton Theological Institution, Alvah Hovey was
nearing the end of a long and distinguished career and Frederick L.
Anderson was gaining in reputation; at Colgate Theological
Seminary, William Newton Clarke was a shining luminary; at
Rochester Theological Seminary, Augustus Hopkins Strong was
at the height of his power and Walter Rauschenbusch had already
made a name for himself; and at Crozer Theological Seminary,
Henry G. Weston, Elias H. Johnson, Milton G. Evans, Henry C.
Vedder, and Alvah S. Hobart were scholars of distinction. But the
greatest concentration of distinguished scholars was at Chicago,
where William Rainey Harper had gathered a group of outstand-
ing Baptist preachers to staff the theological faculty of his new
Baptist super-university. In addition to Harper himself, there were
Ernest DeWitt Burton, Shailer Mathews, Ira M. Price, Edgar J.
Goodspeed, J. M. P. Smith, Charles R. Henderson, Shirley Jackson
Case, Gerald Birney Smith, George Burman Foster, Theodore G.
Soares, and others.

What was true of the theological seminaries was equally true
of the colleges and churches. Throughout the Baptist colleges
there were men of real stature, and in many of the pulpits there
were men of conspicuous ability. Before Rauschenbusch left New
York city in the nineties, he was one of a notable group of young
Baptist ministers which included Leighton Williams and
Nathaniel Schmidt. But there were other more prominent Baptist
ministers in that city; among them were Cortland Myers, Cornelius
Woelfkin, P. S. Henson, W. H. P. Faunce, R. S. MacArthur,
George C. Lorimer, Edward Judson, and William C. Bitting.
Boston and Chicago had their own stars. In Philadelphia, George

Dana Boardman and Russell H. Conwell were men of national reputation. In Rochester, J. W. A. Stewart was pastor of the First Baptist Church, and Clarence A. Barbour, at the Lake Avenue Baptist Church, was gaining fame as the most popular preacher of the college circuit. Moreover, the men of distinction were not limited to the metropolitan centers. There was scarcely a city of any size that could not boast of at least one Baptist minister of scholarly attainment, pulpit eloquence, and literary skill.

These were the men—in seminary, college, and church—who were to determine for the Baptists the shape of things to come.

I

The teachers and preachers of the last decade of the nineteenth century and the first decade of the twentieth century were subjected to a variety of new influences which were to modify and reshape both their inherited faith and their understanding of the church.

The new intellectual currents of the time are familiar enough, having repeatedly been analyzed in detail. New scientific discoveries and hypotheses, most notably Darwin's theory as to the origin of species, posed new problems of biblical interpretation and tended to undermine accepted notions of biblical authority. New methods of textual and historical study raised similar questions and created further uncertainties. The psychology of religion came into its own as a respectable academic discipline. Its analysis of the conversion experience tended to push to one side any emphasis upon the grace of God and the role of the Holy Spirit and centered attention instead on the significance of individual decision and commitment. Sociological studies, initially, were not so disturbing. They were distracting, however, for they emphasized how to get things done by manipulating the external environment. These sociological studies, since they dealt at first hand with everyday aspects of life, were intensely absorbing, and in the end they were to be of crucial significance in suggesting new techniques and a new role for the church.

Despite their eminence, the teachers and preachers of the 1890s were ill-prepared to cope with a headlong rush into a new world. They were able and intelligent, well educated and cultured, and they were earnest and devoted Christians; but their whole religious outlook had been shaped and determined by the basic anti-intellectualism of Evangelicalism. Because Evangelicalism stressed the primacy of personal religious experience, its appeal was directed more to the emotions than to the intellect, and the tendency was to minimize the importance of doctrine and intellectual structure. The traditional language in which the faith had been stated and the old doctrines which had been hammered out in an earlier day were largely retained, and but little effort was expended to relate them to the general currents of thought of the time. Thus Christians came more and more to live in three worlds: the world of their everyday life, the world of their religious experience, and the world of their inherited religious faith. Far from provoking Christians to rethink their position, the contradictions implicit in their endeavor to live in three worlds were largely bypassed, and scarcely any real attempt was made to reconstruct a coherent and systematic body of doctrine. To engage in any such enterprise, it was assumed, could only result in diverting attention from the main task, which was to win a simple and clear-cut emotional decision for Christ.

By the nineties, however, the new intellectual currents were presenting such a sharp challenge to the old doctrines that they could no longer be ignored. Unfortunately, impelled by the necessity to restate the Christian faith in terms that would be intellectually defensible and convincing, the leaders of the churches were inclined to forget that the Christian faith had any claim of its own to truth. Having been schooled to regard the subtleties of theological discussion with distaste, they were ill-prepared to do much more than to appropriate uncritically the conclusions of supposedly objective scholarship. The theologians in the seminaries strove manfully to do more than this, as is amply evidenced in the repeated editions of their systematic theologies. They responded in various ways to the problem, but the demoralizing fact was that the whole apparatus of the inherited doctrinal structure seemed suddenly to have become archaic and completely out of date.

The theological retreat of the 1890s was hastened by the fact that it was an era of complacency for the churches. The frontier had disappeared and the country largely had been "churched." The missionary challenge and stimulus of the West were gone, and the churches in the settled communities and growing cities were well attended and prosperous, and they were preoccupied with building more costly edifices. The economy was expanding and industrial life was booming. To be sure, there were temporary dislocations, but the future seemed bright with promise. Augustus H. Strong, speaking on the subject "Education and Optimism," told the students of Stetson University that there was no room for "gloomy views," and Russell H. Conwell was confident that every man could be and ought to be a millionaire.[1] Among others there was a strong and growing conviction that the techniques of psychology and sociology, if properly utilized, were sufficient to usher in the kingdom. Little wonder that enervation set in, and that the teachers and preachers of the time were in no mood to meet the challenge of the world with a sharp challenge of their own.

Lastly, these teachers and preachers were ill-equipped to deal creatively with the new problems confronting them because their inherited pattern of church life was sustained by no strong theological support. The Baptists had begun as high-churchmen with a closely articulated church life developed in faithfulness and obedience to what they understood to be the clear commands of Christ as set forth in the Scriptures. To be sure, this was not a purely and directly biblically based church life, if such be possible. It was secondary and derivative in the sense that it was undergirded by a tightly knit theological system; by biblical theology, they would have insisted. Thus, the particularities and peculiarities of their church life and church order were derived as much from inferences drawn from their theological understanding as they were from direct biblical precepts. In any event, their pattern of church life was a solid and sturdy structure, carefully defended and strongly supported.

The structure of church life among Baptists was to persist essentially unaltered until the close of the nineteenth century, but as early as the beginning of that century its substructure of theological support was becoming badly eroded. The individualism of the frontier and of the Enlightenment, finding its most conspicuous political and cultural expression in Jeffersonian and Jacksonian democracy, had served to weaken the foundation of Baptist churchmanship; and the definition of the Christian life in purely individualistic terms by Evangelicalism had permitted the crumbling of the foundation to be viewed with relative equanimity.

There were, to be sure, some outward changes. Associational life was allowed slowly to decay and no vigorous associational life was permitted to develop beyond narrow geographical limits. The larger relationship of the churches to each other was improvised on frankly utilitarian grounds, and was then defended on the basis that the Great Commission was spoken to individuals and not to churches. Apart from this, the pattern of local church life remained largely unchanged, and it persisted partly by habit and partly by a continuing conviction that it had been prescribed in the Scriptures. When the authority of the Bible in a literalistic and legalistic sense was brought into question, however, the whole structure toppled almost overnight. Discipline was relaxed, the covenant fell into disuse, the pastoral office was obscured, the deacons were shunted to one side, while boards and committees proliferated. Admission procedures and baptismal practices became lax and indiscriminate; the guarding of the integrity of the Lord's table was forgotten; the covenant meeting was discarded; and the church meeting frayed out in preoccupation with trivialities. The older conception of covenanting with the Lord and with one another to walk together "in all the ways of obedience which He prescribeth," which had been partially replaced by the notion of the church as a purely evangelistic center, was now to give way to an understanding of the church which was defined almost completely in instrumental terms. For some, with the discarding of the older elements of church order, the church became merely a missionary society. For others, the church became a social agency which had to demonstrate its utility by the services it rendered. For still others, the church became a sacramental institution into which an indiscriminate multitude was to be enticed, in the hope that something of the Christian faith would rub off on them.

II

The authority of the Scriptures was the key issue.[2] Augustus H. Strong, Alvah Hovey, Elias H. Johnson, and Henry G. Weston represented what, at first glance, would seem to have been a cautious conservatism. All four, for example, continued to defend close communion. Yet it is obvious that they were confused and demoralized by the impact of the new biblical studies and the new scientific thought, and in various ways they contributed to the easing of the binding force of specific biblical precepts.

In many ways, Strong represented the most valiant attempt to come to terms with the new currents of thought, while still preserving the authority of the Christian Scriptures. He frankly accepted the doctrine of evolution and the methods of biblical criticism. "Neither evolution nor the higher criticism," he said, "has any terrors to one who regards them as parts of Christ's creating and educating process." The composite authorship of the Pentateuch and the existence of two Isaiahs did not disturb him. "Any honest Christian," he affirmed, ". . . has the right to interpret

Jonah and Daniel as allegories rather than histories." The Bible, he insisted, is the record of a progressive revelation, "shaped in human moulds and adapted to ordinary human intelligence." It exhibits "all the personal peculiarities of the writers, together with their defects of culture and literary style." Thus it is a "human composition." And yet, it is also "God's Word," for it "presents to us divine truth in human forms."[3]

Strong was aware of the dangers implicit in the use of historical criticism. The danger, however, stemmed not from the method itself but from the presuppositions of those who used it. He wrote: "The 'historical method' of Scripture interpretation, as it is often employed, ends without Christ because it begins without him." It makes the mistake of "treating Scripture as it would treat any unreligious or heathen literature" and ignores the relationship of Scripture to Christ, who alone furnished the key to its meaning. Properly to interpret the Bible, he insisted, one must adopt a frankly confessional stance which acknowledges as its presuppositions the authority of Christ and the inspiration of Scripture. Then the "historical method" becomes a "servant" and not the "master," showing "not how man made the Scripture for himself, but how God made the Scripture through the imperfect agency of man."[4]

Strong pointed out that the effect of the misuse of the historical method of interpretation upon Baptist churches was "to cut the taproot of their strength and to imperil their very existence."

> Baptist churches are founded upon Scripture. Their doctrine of regenerate church membership, and of church ordinances as belonging only to believers, presupposes an authoritative rule of faith and practice in the New Testament. In controversy with other denominations we have always appealed "to the law and to the testimony."

The authority of the Bible was essential, and this he was willing to defend on the basis of the inspiration of Scripture. "Inspiration," quite obviously to Strong, "did not guarantee inerrancy in things not essential to the main purpose of Scripture," going "no further than to secure a trustworthy transmission by the sacred writers of the truth they were commissioned to deliver." The Scripture writers were neither omniscient nor infallible in all things. Nevertheless, "in spite of its imperfections in matters nonessential to its religious purposes," when properly interpreted, the Bible furnishes "a rule of faith and practice" that is safe, sufficient, and trustworthy.[5]

Alvah Hovey occupied much the same position as did Strong, although his hesitation and uncertainty at numerous points are quite evident. He too accepted the "dynamical" theory of inspiration as most consonant with the evidence turned up by the new biblical studies, but gave it the more precise name of the "religious dynamical" theory of inspiration.[6] He was more confident than Strong, however, that scientific and historical discrepancies could be harmonized by proper interpretation, and he was not so ready to interpret the story of Jonah as allegory rather than historical fact. Still his difference from Strong was only a slight difference in degree of emphasis within a commonly held position.

An entirely different solution to the problem was proposed by William Newton Clarke. His tactic was to surrender all conceptions of a unique biblical authority. The living Christ, he affirmed, was his own witness. "Christ was saving sinners before the New Testament was written, and could do the same today if it had not been written."

> When Christ was departing, he trusted his gospel in the world to the keeping of the Holy Spirit, who was to abide with men. He never promised an infallible church, or an infallible book, or any infallible visible guide, but committed his kingdom to the Spirit and the divine life. Divine Providence brought the Scriptures in as a most valuable help; and they proved so valuable that they have sometimes almost been thought to take the place of the abiding Spirit. . . . Yet Christ was right and wise in trusting his kingdom to the Spirit and the divine life in men. That is where it should be trusted.

What is needed, Clarke insisted, is not truth expressing itself in words but in life: "truth rich, free, spiritual, plentiful, alive, self-imparting." By localizing the authority of Christ in the present activity of the Holy Spirit, however, Clarke reduced almost all outward forms to matters of indifference. In his thought, all notions of church order were dissolved and all that remained was the Church Universal—the communion of the saints—brought into being and sustained by the free agency of the Holy Spirit blowing where it listeth.[7]

Another solution, far removed from the gentle mysticism of Clarke, was represented by some of the men at the University of Chicago, preeminently by Shailer Mathews. "Scientific modernists," they have been called. Despite the magnificent concentration upon biblical study that was so conspicuous there, the Bible came less and less to be regarded as in any sense normative in religion. It was considered a suitable subject for historical study, but the canons of truth were to be found in the sciences; that is to say, in both the older natural sciences and the newer social sciences. So far as religious experience was concerned, the normative discipline was psychology; and so far as the church was concerned, the normative discipline was sociology. It is not surprising, therefore, that in the hands of the men who shared this viewpoint the church increasingly took on the character of a social agency and the real frontier of constructive religious endeavor was thought to be the settlement house.

At Crozer there was the same cautious conservatism that was present at Rochester and Newton, although at all three institutions the younger men were restive. But even Elias Johnson and Henry G. Weston, who stood within the older camp at Crozer, recognized that the "religious dynamical" theory of inspiration advocated by Strong and Hovey was much too easy a solution to the problems that had been raised to be either convincing or defensible. Johnson then proceeded to restate the case for biblical authority in terms that bypassed the debates on the inspiration of the Scriptures. The Bible is authoritative, he insisted, because it bears witness to the central fact of God's revelation in Christ, and this witness is sufficiently clear to make preoccuption with theories of inspiration both fruitless and unnecessary.

> It is of no small moment that we should avoid the common error of attaching undue importance to the theories about inspiration. It is a matter of speculative rather than practical interest. . . . It is admitted that complete revelation was afforded in the person of Jesus Christ; that the Holy Spirit conferred on the apostles insight sufficient to acquaint them with all either they or we need to know concerning Christ; and that such aid as this qualified them to tell what they knew.

Weston seems to have shared this point of view, for he emphasized that the Bible, after all, was a book of principles, rather than a book of rules or a code of laws. He was ready to defend the traditional Baptist pattern of church order, but he confessed that this could be done only on the basis of general theological principles, rather than specific biblical precepts.[8]

III

Of all the men of the 1890s and early 1900s, Augustus H. Strong and Henry G. Weston provided the most completely thought out and carefully articulated statements of Baptist ecclesiology. Strong recognized that the word "church" was used with two distinct meanings in the New Testament. "In its largest signification," he said, it means "the whole company of regenerate persons in all times and ages." In this large sense, the church is "the body of Christ—the organism to which he gives spiritual life and through which he manifests the fulness of his power and grace." The New Testament, however, distinguishes "between this invisible or universal church and the individual church in which the universal church takes local and temporal form, and in which the idea of the church as a whole is concretely exhibited." The "sole object" of "the local church is the glory of God in the complete establishment of his kingdom, both in the hearts of believers and in the world." Since there is a "transcendent element" in the church, and since "it is the great company of persons whom Christ has saved, in whom he dwells, to whom and through whom he reveals God," the church "cannot be defined in merely human terms as an aggregate of individuals associated for social, benevolent, or even spiritual purposes." On the other hand, unlike other divine institutions such as the family and the state, membership in the church is neither hereditary nor compulsory, but is rather an expression of an "inward and conscious reception of Christ and his truth." In this sense, the church is a voluntary society, but Strong cites with approval A. J. Gordon's contention that the definition of the church as "a voluntary association of believers, united together for purposes of worship and edification" is both inadequate and misleading. "It is no more true than that hands and feet are voluntarily united in the human body for purposes of locomotion and work. The church is formed from within. Christ, present by the Holy Ghost, regenerating men by the sovereign action of the Spirit and organizing them into himself as the living center, is the only principle that can explain the existence of the church."[9]

With regard to the outward life of the church, Strong rejected the notion that "the church is an exclusively spiritual body, destitute of all formal organization and bound together only by the mutual relation of each believer to his indwelling Lord." He rejected also "the theory that the form of church organization is not definitely prescribed in the New Testament, but is a matter of expediency, each body of believers being permitted to adopt that method of organization which best suits its circumstances and condition." He believed, as Weston would also, that the proper order of the church had been prescribed "in all essential particulars" in the New Testament. He was somewhat more confident than Weston would be, however, that there were specific laws, rather than general principles; but this was largely a semantic difference. Christ, he insisted, is the only lawgiver, and thus the government of the church partakes of the nature of an absolute monarchy. "In ascertaining the will of Christ, however, and in applying his commands to providential exigencies, the Holy Spirit enlightens one member through the counsel of another and, as the result of combined deliberation, guides the whole body to right conclusions." In this sense, with regard to the interpretation and execution of Christ's will by the body, the church is a democracy.[10]

The two offices which are of divine institution and essential to the being of a particular church are those of pastor (otherwise called bishop or elder) and deacon. The pastor is a "spiritual teacher," the "administrator of the ordinances," and the "superintendent of discipline, as well as presiding officer at the meetings of the church." Strong is somewhat troubled by the connotations of the concept that the pastor is to "rule" in the church. The pastor, to be sure, must "take responsibility to put himself forward when there is need, but he is to *rule* only by moral suasion, and that only by guiding, teaching, and carrying into effect the rules imposed by Christ and the decisions of the church in accordance with those rules." This, of course, is what Baptists always meant by the concept of the "pastoral ruler." His function, as Strong points out, was "not legislative but executive," and it was within this context that he was to admonish, govern, and rule. Strong's view of the office of deacon may have been somewhat broader than Weston's, for he thought of the deacon as a helper to the pastor and the church in spiritual as well as in temporal things. Strong noted, however, that C. H. Spurgeon had secured "spiritual helpers" at the Metropolitan Tabernacle in London by having the church elect "elders" to "attend to the spiritual affairs of the church" in the same manner that the deacons "attend to the temporal affairs."[11]

Strong gave major attention to the relationship of local churches to each other. "The general nature of this relation," he observed, "is that of fellowship between equals." On the one hand, there is an "absolute equality of the churches"; on the other hand, there must be "fraternal fellowship and co-operation." Stated another way, "independence is qualified by interdependence," and it is the duty of ministers to teach the members of their churches "the larger unity of the whole church of God." The fraternal fellowship of churches involves, among other things, "the duty of special consultation with regard to matters affecting the common interest." This, in turn, involves "the duty of seeking advice" and "the duty of taking advice."

Strong was moving in the direction of the stronger connectionalism that was characteristic of the earlier Baptists, and he observed that "the polity of the New Testament is congregational rather than independent." He was not quite sure, however, what form the closer connectionalism should take. The associations had been stripped of their functions both by the voluntary societies that had been formed and by the substitution of councils to handle matters of ecclesiastical concern. Strong mentioned that H. O. Rowlands had urged "the giving up of special Councils and the turning of the Association into a Permanent Council . . . to consider and judge such questions as may be referred to it by individual churches." There were several advantages to be gained. The association "could revise and rescind its action, whereas the present Council when once adjourned can never be called together again." Furthermore, "this method would prevent the packing of a Council, and the Council when once constituted would have greater influence." Strong's counsel with reference to this proposal was one of caution. "We feel slow to sanction such a plan, not only for the reason that it seems destitute of New Testament authority and example, but because it tends toward a Presbyterian form of government. All permanent bodies of this sort gradually arrogate to themselves power; indirectly if not directly they can assume original jurisdiction; their decisions have altogether too much infiuence, if they go further than personal persuasion."[12]

Henry G. Weston's views concerning the church paralleled quite closely those of Strong. He also began with the distinction between the two New Testament usages of the word "church." It is used to denote the whole body of Christians and it is used to refer to "a local individual body—a visible organization." Weston was very clear in his insistence that the church, when the term is used in the first sense, "differs radically and generically from all other organizations." The following quotation aptly expresses this idea of the nature of the church:

> It is not a development of the moral, religious, or social nature of man; it is not a product of the human intellect; it is not a school of opinion, nor a voluntary association of persons of similar tastes or pursuits. It is a supernatural and vital union, a new creation, a divine organism.

Thus defined, the church is a body of Christ, performing "the same offices in the world which Christ performed." It is "Christ's temple; his habitation; his chosen dwelling place, where God reveals his presence, is worshipped, and bestows his blessing." Weston was equally clear that the church as "a body of professed believers in Christ, baptized on a credible confession of faith in him, associated for worship, work, and discipline," was an expression, however inadequate, of the life that was to be found in the larger or universal church. These churches, furthermore, were under perpetual obligation to perform two acts of Christ's institution, baptism and the communion, which commemorate and declare the gospel.[13]

When Weston moved from what he called the essential constitution of the church to matters of polity or church order, his analysis was no less incisive. He acknowledged that a New Testament polity is not to "be found detailed in rigid, minute, and unvarying directions in the New Testament." If the church is to have "life and growth, it must necessarily have a form flexible and variant, the variations never departing from the essentials of Christianity, but caused and determined by them."

> There are two opposite errors on this subject against which we must guard. The first is, that there is no church polity obligatory on Christians; the second, that everything in church life is so ordained in the New Testament that in every church, everywhere, and in all time, minute particulars must be identical.

Since a church is "the organic realization of the divine life," its shape must be consonant with the essential genius of its inner life and therefore must be determined by theological principles. Thus there is an intimate connection between faith and practice.

> A given theology and a given polity are rarely dissociated. The external constitution of a church is the fruit and exponent of its inner principle of belief, while "the outward form and constitution of a church, its worship and discipline, its offices, its ritual, react with great force on its inner life and on the doctrine which it teaches." A scheme of doctrine leads to a cognate theory of the church.

Because of this reciprocal relationship, Weston insisted, questions of polity must be decided with great care, it being both irrational and unscriptural to regard them as matters of relative indifference.[14]

On the basis of the biblical testimony, Weston formulated four theological principles "which must be conserved and developed in all church polity," principles which "lie at the very source and center" of the church's life.

1. The vital relation of Christ to each member and of each member to Christ. Each member sustains as close a relation to Christ as any other member; there is an essential and vital equality of the members, so that there can be no sacerdotal class, no class with special privileges, or permitted any special access to Christ, or endowed with any special function. The members of the church are all kings and priests.

2. The living and continuous relation of Christ to the church. The life of the church is not something deposited, a store of grace to be distributed by the officers or received in the sacraments; it is a living Christ, a person and a presence to whom the church is united as the body is united to the head; as the branches are united to the vine.

3. The organic relation of members to one another and to the body. They are one, not by voluntary combination, but by a common birth, a common nature, and a common life.

4. The completeness of each church; first, as related to Christ; second, as related to one another; third, as related to the world.

These four principles, said Weston, may briefly be summarized as a living Savior, a living church, an organic church, and a complete church.[15]

Questions of polity and church order, however, are not to be decided solely on the basis of general theological principles. In addition to necessary deductions from admitted scriptural principles, Weston pointed out that there are other more specific guides to ecclesiastical construction in the New Testament which may not be disregarded and which must be taken seriously. These consist of express biblical precepts, apostolic example, and "the practice of the primitive churches while under apostolic directions." But these specific guides must all be examined in the light of general theological considerations to determine whether or not they "rest upon a principle common to all men in all conditions, or on principles or facts peculiar to certain men, to certain times, and to certain circumstances." In other words, it is necessary to "distinguish between that which belongs to the church and that which belongs to a church; between that which is clearly permanent and that which as clearly belongs to the formative period." Above all, these specific guides must be understood, interpreted, and applied in terms that are consonant with the essential constitution of the church and the theological principles derived therefrom.[16]

It is in this setting that Weston discusses the detailed questions of church order, and for the most part his conclusions are quite traditional. The bishop or presbyter, for example, is not only to be a preacher, teacher, shepherd, and leader; he is also to "rule."

Deacons, likewise, retain responsibility for the temporal affairs of the church, being commissioned "to serve the church in all ways" which do not "fall within the province of the bishop." One curious feature of Weston's exposition of his ecclesiology, in view of his insistence upon the organic relationship of Christians to one another, is the complete absence of any discussion of the association. This, quite obviously, was the result of a conflict between his third and fourth principles. It was a conflict which he never attempted to resolve. Churches could give expression to their relationship to each other, he insisted, only through informal councils which may be convened at the request of a church to give advice on a particular issue.[17]

IV

Weston, by appealing more explicitly to general doctrinal concepts than to specific biblical precepts, was more successful than Strong in providing a defensible biblical grounding for the traditional ecclesiological convictions and practices of Baptists. As has been noted, however, the younger men at Crozer and Rochester were restive and were looking elsewhere for guidance. The future, so far as these men were concerned, lay either with the gentle mysticism of William Newton Clarke at Colgate or with the "scientific modernism" of Shailer Mathews at Chicago. The effect of both these positions, as we have seen, was to dissolve any concept of the church as distinct from a social agency and to reduce all questions of church order to merely pragmatic considerations. Actually the door was already open to ecclesiastical innovations and improvisation, for the notion of a structured church life had been badly undermined during the course of the nineteenth century.

The older Baptist pattern of church order was much more seriously eroded than the thought of either Strong or Weston would indicate. The radical individualism of Jeffersonian democracy, which had found expression in Backus, Leland, and Wayland, had deeply penetrated Baptist life and had been reinforced by the general temper of Evangelicalism. While this influence can be seen in both Strong and Weston, the attrition to which the older concepts had been subjected by this individualistic emphasis is much more apparent in the formulations of Alvah Hovey.

In his *Manual of Christian Theology*, Hovey dismisses the concept of the universal church as being without any real significance. He notes that the word is used a "few times" in the New Testament to denote "all Christians in heaven and on earth," but insists that this is an "exceptional" usage that has no bearing on the constitution or government of the church. Even in terms of a particular church, Hovey's whole mood is permissive. "The members of a Christian church, fully organized for growth and service, may be divided into three classes, laical, diaconal, and clerical," but it is the body alone that is essential, and not the body and its duly appointed officers.

The pastors of the churches are to be "leaders, teachers, and examples to the flock in all spiritual things," but their only authority is "moral . . . depending on their character, their call from God, their Christian knowledge, and their position as religious teachers." Under ordinary circumstances, he observes, pastors are likely "to have all the respect and confidence which they deserve."

The deacons are "to assist the pastor in the subordinate duties of his office," and thus their duties are of "a semi-spiritual character," being determined by "the amount of help which the pastor needs." There is no adequate evidence, Hovey maintains, that the deacons ought to have charge of the finances of the church. Consequently, "a church may select for its treasurer one who is not a deacon or may appoint a financial committee to look after pecuniary matters." Indeed, in small churches there may be no need to have deacons, since their only function is to assist the pastor and in a small church the pastor may be able to discharge all his responsibilities himself. Nevertheless, "it would be wise, even in such cases, to have at least one deacon who can take the lead should the office of pastor become vacant."

The "lay members" of the church are required "to see that their pastor has reasonable compensation for his official work," but in case they refuse to contribute, there is little reason to suppose that the church has the right to deal with the delinquents by way of discipline.

The churches are "organically separate," but they "ought to respect the action of one another." They may, and sometimes it is highly desirable that they should, seek advice from several churches gathered by their representatives in a council; and upon a voluntary basis they "may combine their resources and influence for the furtherance of religious or benevolent enterprises."[18]

The permissiveness of Hovey, which was always interpreted as safeguarding the "rights" of the individual member and the individual church, was closely related to what E. Y. Mullins identified as the constitutive principle of Baptist church life, i.e., the competency, under God, of the individual soul in religion. To the extent that Baptists were to develop an apologetic for their church life during the early decades of the twentieth century, it was to be on the basis of this highly individualistic principle. It has become increasingly apparent that this principle was derived from the general cultural and religious climate of the nineteenth century rather than from any serious study of the Bible. But it was its inadequacy as a basis for church life, rather than its point of origin, that constituted a major problem for Baptists. Not only did it fail to provide detailed guidance for questions of church order beyond such generalized corollary axioms as "all believers have a right to interpret the Bible for themselves" and "all believers have a right to equal privileges in the church"; but also it served to dissolve any real concept of the church, for it interpreted the faith as a one-to-one relationship between God and the individual.

The practical effect of the stress upon "soul competency" as the cardinal doctrine of Baptists was to make every man's hat his own church. This concept was made quite explicit by W. R. McNutt, who from 1928 until his retirement in 1944 was Professor of Practical Theology in Crozer Theological Seminary. In his book, *Polity and Practice in Baptist Churches*,[19] he asserted that the "directive life principle" of Baptist polity is "the creative idea that the individual is competent in all matters of religion" and "has within himself by divine gift and right those capacities that make him competent to meet all the demands with which genuine religion confronts him." Thus the individual "has no inescapable need of church to bring him salvation or to mediate to him divine grace." He stands alone, since "competency reposes authority in religion within the individual."

> It sets each man on a throne which holds absolute sway over his own realm. And he may not, for any reason, abdicate; he rules by divine right and appointment.

He also stands free and unfettered, since "the soul that is competent is likewise free." Competency and freedom "cannot be separated in thought, and must not be divorced in organized religion." Any abridgment or denial of "the exercise of soul liberty" can only serve "to strangle man and fly into the face of God."[20]

A church, said McNutt, comes into being as the result of a subordinate principle. It is the principle of "the free association of believers." While an individual may not abdicate either his authority or his freedom, "he may call to his side those who have counsel to give" and "from them take little or much, as seems good in his sight." This "free association of believers" is useful also "to keep their hearts warm in allegiance to him, their Lord, to culture their souls in his graces, and to spread the good news about him through all the earth." Thus a church is no more than a voluntary association "constituted by individuals who believe themselves endowed with competency in religion," and it is "brought into being for the furtherance of their purposes." It seemed quite clear to McNutt that "such a church, by the very logic of its nature, must behave democratically." Any other type of organization would violate its "inherent constitution."

> If the individual member is to grow, he must have large scope in which to exercise his soul competency. Young eagles cannot learn to fly when confined in a cage. . . . No more can the young Christian be expected to grow when the wings of his free soul are hurt by the scissors born of laws and the inhibitions begotten of fears. No authority, therefore, which may be conceived to interfere with healthbegetting freedom can be at all permitted. Such organization or polity as does come into being by sheer necessity of group purpose must rest lightly as the dawn upon the vibrant, naked soul of the individual. He is master of all polity and must never be mastered by it. Polity is made for man and not man for polity. He that was created in the image of God must not be bound by the cords of organization.

As each individual is "competent," so each church is "competent in and of itself." Each church is regarded "as a law unto itself." Nevertheless, each church as an "independent unit" may function voluntarily and democratically "in co-operation with other groups of disciples to enlarge the reign of God in the hearts of men everywhere."[21]

While McNutt was emphatic and uncompromising in his statement of what seemed to him to be the clear position of Baptists with regard to the church, he recognized that the position was not without its difficulties, and a curious note of ambiguity was introduced when he looked to the future. He confessed that, as a result of the findings of the psychologists and sociologists, "clear thinking reveals no such thing as the *individual* in society, neither can it discover the strictly *independent* church." Furthermore, it was quite apparent that the churches themselves had "found it impossible to live, much less to grow, in isolation." This movement away from their "ideal" had been "painful to many Baptists," but they were powerless to resist it. They have, to be sure, "sought steadfastly to actualize in practice what they proclaim in theory," but it has been a losing struggle.

> As human society in which the churches live has grown increasingly complex in all its manifestations, so have the churches grown more complex in polity. Such lies as a necessity in the very nature of the aim of the churches, which, as we understand it, is to break the bread of life to a needy world. To do this, complexity must be matched by adequate complexity—which means a more involved polity or method of acting. But in this movement, be it noted, the structural simplicities of pure democracy and complete independency have been supplemented by more involved items of polity. Some are inclined to slur these creations as "machinery," or "overhead machinery." As a matter of fact, however, they are but further adaptations of living churches to new conditions and demands.

We must not, however, be unduly disturbed by this development. We must remember, said McNutt, that "as polity cannot claim to be an end in itself, neither can democracy or independency." They are "creative ideals" and not "hoops of steel," and if the new ways "tend to make more swift the feet of them who run therein as promoters of the King's business," they are justified and worthy of the churches.[22]

The one thing that is apparent, whether one looks to Clarke, Mathews, Hovey, or McNutt, is the fact that none of them had clear words of guidance for the task of ecclesiastical construction. As they saw it, the churches of the twentieth century were on their own, free to experiment and to improvise to their heart's content on a purely pragmatic basis, quite divorced from any theological or biblical considerations.

NOTES

[1] Augustus H., Strong, *Miscellanies*. 2 vols. (Philadelphia: 1912), I, pp. 172-196. Also Winthrop S. Hudson, *The Great Tradition of the American Churches* (New York, 1953), pp. 182-185.

[2] The shifting views toward biblical authority among Baptists is discussed at length by Norman H. Maring in *Foundations*, vol. 1, no. 3 (July, 1958), p. 52; and vol. 1, no. 4 (October, 1958), p. 30.

[3] Augustus H. Strong, *Outlines of Systematic Theology* (Philadelphia, 1903), pp. ix, 55, 58 ff. Also Augustus H. Strong, *Tour of Missions* (Philadelphia, 1918), p. 186.

[4] Strong, *Outlines*, pp. xi, 55-60. Also *Tour of Missions;* pp. 177, 181, 186-187, 203.

[5] Strong, *Outlines*, pp. 59-60, 62. Also *Tour of Missions*, p. 191.

[6] Alvah Hovey, *Manual of Christian Theology* (New York, 1900), pp. 83, 85.

[7] William Newton Clarke, *An Outline of Christian Theology* (New York, 1898), pp. 38, 46, 381-385; see also pp. 41-45, 49 ff.

[8] E. H. Johnson, *An Outline of Systematic Theology* (Philadelphia, 1895), pp. 34, 350.

[9] Strong, *Systematic Theology* (Philadelphia, 1907); Twentieth Printing, 1958; III, pp. 887-889, 893.

[10] *Ibid.*, pp. 895-897, 903.

[11] *Ibid.*, pp. 916-918.

[12] *Ibid.*, pp. 926-929.

[13] Henry G. Weston, *Constitution and Polity of the New Testament Church* (Philadelphia, 1895), pp. 17, 18, 20.

[14] *Ibid.*, pp. 47, 48.

[15] *Ibid.*, pp. 48 ff.

[16] *Ibid.*, pp. 49 ff.

[17] *Ibid.*, pp. 61-63, 68-69, 73-76.

[18] Hovey, *op. cit.*, pp. 347, 351-354, 357.

[19] W. R. McNutt, *Polity and Practice in Baptist Churches* (Valley Forge: Judson Press, 1935, 1959), pp. 21-24. Used by permission.

[20] *Ibid.*, pp. 21-24.

[21] *Ibid.*, pp. 25-29.

[22] *Ibid.*, pp. 29-30, 32-33.

Afterword

The essays brought together in this book deal with, among other aspects of Baptist life, a continuing tension between freedom and authority, independence and interdependence, individual autonomy and corporate responsibility. Quite inadvertently they fit together in rather surprising fashion to exhibit varied facets of a common focus over a chronological period ranging from Baptist beginnings in America to the early decades of the twentieth century.

Given the endemic individualism of the American scene, it is not surprising that the delicate balance early Baptists sought to maintain between the two extremes tended to tilt in the direction of individual freedom, independence, and autonomy at the expense of communal restraint and responsibility. This tilt was often more true of Baptist rhetoric than it was of Baptist practice. Structural expressions of interdependence in Baptist institutional arrangements did not wholly disappear and served to counterbalance the push toward an uninhibited individualism. Controls also were maintained by the pervasive influence of a few exceptionally strong leaders and by widespread acceptance of principles and doctrines promulgated in printed materials circulated throughout the churches both in the north and the south, among black as well as white congregations, by the American Baptist Publication Society.

The strong rhetorical stress on freedom, independence, soul liberty, and the right of private judgment did not present a great problem in maintaining unity among most Baptists in America. It is true that the new evangelical theology of the late eighteenth century and the first half of the nineteenth century did produce three spin-offs of some consequence and that the slavery controversy did result in a major division. It also is true that black

Baptists coalesced in separate churches and conventions of their own following the Civil War. But in only one of these divisions was local autonomy a major issue. Moreover, within these several groupings a remarkable unanimity prevailed, and a heightened unity and even centralization began to develop. This was notably true of Southern Baptists, almost equally true of various formerly "foreign-language" groups, and only slightly less so of the black Baptist community. The old-line American (Northern) Baptists exhibited considerable cohesiveness throughout the nineteenth century, but in the twentieth century they were to be torn by theological controversy. These Northern Baptists compounded their problem when they attempted to utilize the rhetoric and practice of autonomy and freedom as a means of preserving unity in the midst of differences of opinion about the mission of the church.

I

Southern Baptists by the middle decades of the twentieth century had resolved, to the satisfaction of most of their number, the tension that had been present among Baptists from their earliest years in America. In spite of slogans to the contrary, Southern Baptists by the third decade of the twentieth century had achieved a remarkable degree of cohesiveness and centralized authority. There were some notable exceptions, but in most Southern Baptist congregations and in the formal stance of their theological seminaries unusual deference was yielded to programs and directives emanating from Nashville, from the twin power centers of Southern Baptist life—the Executive Committee of the Convention and the Sunday School Board. The operation of the Convention itself was highly integrated and allowed little room for independent maneuver. State conventions were technically as independent as local congregations, but they exhibited little inclination to pursue a wayward course.

The centralization so evident among Southern Baptists was accomplished without much reflection. Seldom was any searching biblical and theological analysis and discussion given primary consideration as justification for what had taken place. Indeed, what talk there was continued to be in terms of local autonomy, soul liberty, and the right of private judgment. The cohesion and consensus among Southern Baptists evolved out of what may be termed "nontheological factors." Among these factors, priority must be given to an ecclesiastical structure, dating back beyond

1845, which placed boards and agencies (including theological seminaries) directly under the control of the Southern Baptist Convention. Thus centralization did not appear, as it was to appear in the north, as an innovation counter to a tradition of independent "societies" and independent theological seminaries. A second cohesive factor was a regional self-consciousness and a developing southern "mystique" which served both as a bond of loyalty and as a sanction for a southern style of church life and way of doing things. The third factor strengthening consensus and centralization was a programmatic pragmatism taught by Professor Gaines Dobbins in the seminary at Louisville and put into practice by the Sunday School Board. Dobbins' mentor was John Dewey, and the justification for insisting upon strict adherence to the details of convention-wide programming was the contention that the programs when followed without modification "worked" and produced results. Uniform practice, in turn, accentuated the existing cohesion.

Black Baptists maintained unity not so much through formal structures as through the isolation imposed by patterns of segregation, through evolving features of worship and religious life sanctified as an integral part of the black experience, and through the influence exerted by charismatic leaders. The pivotal role of these charismatic leaders meant that personality clashes became an important factor in the struggles leading to separation into two, then three, national black Baptist conventions. Principles were involved and constitutional questions were precipitating factors, but the debate was not so much over issues of polity as it was over breaches of constitutional provisions. It was at this point that the personality clashes occurred.

The cohesion of smaller Baptist groups has been remarkable. Some have been theologically based, but even the Seventh-day Baptists cling together as much as a result of family tradition and of an intimate family spirit made possible by their limited numbers as by strong doctrinal conviction. The "foreign language" Baptists, even after the loss of the language which brought them into existence, continue to exhibit unity and cohesion, being held together more by lingering ethnic ties than by formal ecclesiological understandings. Leaders, who have gained the respect and esteem of the members of these smaller groups, also played an important part in the ability of the smaller Baptist bodies to hold together, maintain their unity, and survive.

In contrast to most other Baptist groups, American Baptists in the north encountered a time of troubles as the twentieth century advanced, being beset with controversy and threatened with disintegration. It was a confusing time, for each camp in the convention simultaneously adopted contradictory positions on the issue of centralized authority as groups sought to deal with their respective concerns.

II

The American Baptist Churches in the U.S.A., known for the first four decades of its existence as the Northern Baptist Convention, dates from 1907 when a meeting was summoned to devise a plan for coordinating the work of the several national "societies," such as the American Baptist Home Mission Society, the American Baptist Foreign Mission Society, and the American Baptist Publication Society.[1] The formation of the convention was also in part a response to the insistence of the Southern Baptist Convention that there be a regional allocation of territory.[2] Furthermore, by combining "the May meetings" of the constituent societies within the framework of a convention meeting at the same time and place, an opportunity would be afforded for those in attendance to voice collectively the conscience of the churches on issues of general moral concern. Every assurance was given, however, that the convention would in no way compromise the independence of the national societies or of the local churches.

The continuing independence of the societies was, in any ultimate sense, a fiction. The voting membership of the societies was identical with that of the convention at its annual meeting so that there was no realistic possibility for a society to withdraw from its convention affiliation. These same voting members of the convention also elected the members of the societies' boards of managers and by the selection of board members were able to control policy. Furthermore, the budget or finance committee, overseeing the disbursement of jointly raised funds, exercised real authority through its responsibility for the allocation of funds to the different societies.

Two features of American Baptists are worthy of comment. First, the Convention had no control over theological seminaries. Each seminary was free to pursue its own independent course. Second, while there was an *esprit de corps* among the churches, the lack of a central denominational agency minimized the development of informal controls centered in and around uniform denominational programming. This feeling of independence by local churches remained undiminished during the brief interval before the convention began to be torn by controversy. For the individual pastor, his pulpit was his throne to the extent that he could win the support of his own congregation.

Within this context, it is not surprising to discover that American Baptists had few rivals, other than Congregationalists, in spearheading the liberalizing tendencies in American Protestantism during the first decades of the twentieth century. American Baptist theological seminaries — Colgate, Crozer, Rochester, and the Divinity School of the University of Chicago—led the way with a galaxy of theologians, such as William Newton Clarke, Walter Rauschenbusch, Shailer Mathews, and many others of equal stature. The seminary professors were joined by a notable and growing number of pastors in cities and towns throughout the land who were leading their congregations into new ways of understanding the Christian faith. Nor, on the other hand, is it surprising to discover that Baptists supplied many of the most conspicuous leaders of the vigorous counterattack to preserve what they regarded as the "fundamentals" of the faith, men such as W. B. Riley, John Roach Straton, and two pastors imported from the south and Canada—J. Frank Norris and T. T. Shields. Other leaders, more moderate and less conspicuous, were perhaps in the long run more influential.

The controversy which raged among American Baptists from around 1917 to 1947, diverting attention from almost every other concern, had its curious aspect. Leaders of a liberal persuasion were in control of the then Northern Baptist Convention from the outset, and with some concessions they managed to retain control throughout the period which ended with the final fundamentalist defection following the 1946 Grand Rapids meeting of the Convention. As a consequence of this control, fundamentalist leaders focused their attack, on the one hand, against all centralizing tendencies which invaded the rights of independent local congregations. They spoke much of the betrayal of conscience when funds from local congregations were used to finance policies which were at variance with what these congregations believed to be central to the Christian faith. At the same time, on the other hand, fundamentalist leaders carried on a running battle to establish centralized control over all aspects of denominational life. They insisted that theological seminaries be brought under Convention control and that a creedal test be imposed on members of theological faculties, as well as on

Convention missionaries, delegates, officers, and board members, and even upon local churches if they were to retain membership in the Convention.

Leaders of a liberal persuasion were involved in a similar bifurcated advocacy. They had been promoters and defenders of the centralizing tendency represented by the Convention, believing it to be a means of making the work of the societies more efficient and effective. At the same time, as a means of deflecting fundamentalist attempts to take control of the Convention by imposing creedal tests, they invoked the historic Baptist emphasis on soul liberty, the right of private judgment, and the independence of the local church.

Small wonder that W. R. McNutt was of divided mind in 1935 when he discussed the major features of Baptist polity and practice. McNutt was clearheaded enough to recognize that sociologists and psychologists had made it plain that neither individuals nor churches can exist in isolation and that strictly speaking there can be no such thing as an *individual* in society or a wholly *independent* church.[3] Writing in a time of swirling controversy, however, McNutt was inhibited from abandoning the old slogans of independency in any attempt to work out a more adequate and defensible ecclesiology, for he believed that the Northern Baptist Convention could be held together only by allowing considerable latitude with respect to theological views. The Convention was held together but not without defections taking place at both ends of the theological spectrum. At one end two new Baptist groups came into existence; at the other end defection was marked by quiet departures to other and more peaceful churches.

III

American Baptists did not enjoy sufficient tranquillity even to discuss the anomalies of their Convention structure until after 1947 when the Conservative Baptist Association was organized with its constituent churches formally severing their previous affiliation with the American Baptist Convention. Throughout the period of turbulence, as Theron Chastain noted, it was regarded as "too dangerous to engage in such discussions," for "any criticism of the denomination was looked upon as a threat to its existence," so great was the fear of disintegration.[4] There had been some tinkering over the years, to be sure, with greater efficiency being sought in 1920 through a Board of General Promotion which was replaced four years later by a Board of Missionary Cooperation.

This board, in turn, was supplanted in 1934 by a General Council and a Council on Finance and Promotion. In 1944, at the instigation of Luther Wesley Smith, the American Baptist Publication Society and the Board of Education were merged and renamed the Board of Education and Publication. There had not been, however, any thoroughgoing reappraisal of the work of the Convention and of its internal organizational relationships as well as its relationship to affiliated agencies, such as state conventions and city societies. Even after 1947 it took several years for Convention officers to realize that even tentative steps toward reappraisal and reorganization could be taken, and it took even longer for them to become adjusted to the idea that theological discussion could now take place without creating mutual recriminations, ill-feeling, and further rifts.

The first step was a modest one—the appointment in 1950 of a general secretary of the denomination. Also in that year the name was changed from Northern to American Baptist Convention. Added denominational cohesion was sought by adopting *The Crusader* as an official convention-wide newspaper. The next step began in 1952 with a series of studies conducted by the General Council with the aim of securing greater coordination among Convention agencies by adjustments in denominational machinery. An outside management survey, not a theological review, led to the strengthening of the General Council, the realignment and consolidation of Convention agencies, and the housing of them in a single headquarters building. An attempt was made to carry over these moves toward centralization into a reorganization of field operations. However, these proposals ran counter to a developing interest in a representational system through which authority would ascend from the churches to determine national policy.

IV

The counter movement had been developing for some years. It was rooted in a reawakened theological interest in the church and its mission. At the insistence of Edwin T. Dahlberg and Eugene M. Austin, the General Council had approved the suggestion that the time had come for American Baptists to stop avoiding theological discussion. Within an administrative group which hitherto had regarded theological questions as too divisive to be allowed to surface, the decision to hold a theological conference in 1954 at Green Lake signaled a marked change in the climate of opinion among American Baptists. Responsibility for making arrangements was vested in the staff of the Board of Education and Publication, the first conference was astonishingly successful, and in 1956 it was followed by six equally successful regional conferences. Three years later a second national conference dealt specifically with the doctrine of the church. This conference was preceded by preparatory study groups throughout the country, and the resource papers for the study groups were later published under the title *Baptist Concepts of the Church* (Judson Press, 1959).

For the next seven or eight years the issue of representative government within the Convention, most often in the form of discussion of the associational principle, was a recurring theme of articles and editorials in *Foundations,* a quarterly which had begun publication in 1958. The grass-roots character of this interest in the association and associational representation was manifest during these years by numerous experiments in reorganization and revitalizing of local associations. At the same time, some state conventions were moving in this direction as they began to restructure their organization.

This developing interest in representation led to the appointment in 1968 of a Study Commission on Denominational Structure (SCODS) with a mandate to develop a more representative structure with clear lines of accountability. When the commission reported in 1970, its first recommendation was a shift in name from the American Baptist Convention to the American Baptist Churches, a shift designed to emphasize that the membership was churches, not an assembly of individuals, while indicating their independence as well as their interdependence within a more tightly knit organization. Proposals for organizational change included substituting a biennial for the traditional annual "convention" or meeting of delegates from the churches, and transferring much of the legislative function to a General Board of 170 members. Almost three-fours (123) of the members of the General Board were to be elected by delegates to election districts grouped within region-state-city areas, with 41 being elected by the national biennial meeting and the remaining 6 being the elected general officers of the American Baptist Churches.[5]

The thrust of the SCODS proposals, which were adopted in 1972, was to recover the balance between independence and interdependence by combining authority with accountability and by seeking to achieve unity without a completely centralized consolidation. Such a delicate balance is difficult to maintain. The tendency always is to tilt in one direction or the other. Executive committees tend to accumulate authority by neglecting and ignoring procedures of accountability, while dispersed units of administration (including local churches) often tend to become unduly self-assertive at the expense of structures designed to express and promote unity. Even the most carefully devised structure is unlikely to provide cohesion unless it is undergirded by the consensus of a common purpose, by a commonly accepted style of doing things arising from common programming, and by loyalty engendered by respected and esteemed leaders. For Baptists in transition, these are considerations to be kept in mind that are quite as important as formal structure and organization.

NOTES

[1] Other societies included within the Convention framework were the Woman's American Baptist Home Mission Society, Woman's American Baptist Foreign Mission Society, and the American Baptist Historical Society.

[2] See Donnell R. Harris, "The Gradual Separation of Southern and Northern Baptists, 1845-1907," *Foundations*, vol. 7, no. 2 (1964), pp. 130-144.

[3] William Roy McNutt, *Polity and Practice in Baptist Churches* (Valley Forge: Judson Press, 1935, 1959), p. 29.

[4] Theron Chastain, "The Dynamics of American Baptist Denominational Life," *Foundations*, vol. 4, no. 1 (1961), p. 292.

[5] The SCODS proposals were summarized by Glenn Asquith, Jr., *Foundations*, vol. 15, no. 1 (1972), pp. 36-39. The SCODS reorganization was subsequently refined in accordance with recommendations brought in by a Study Commission on Organizational Relationships (SCOR).

Index